MUTUAL FUND INVESTING ON THE INTERNET

MUTUAL FUND INVESTING ON THE INTERNET

PETER G. CRANE

AP Professional

AP Professional is a Division of Academic Press

Boston   San Diego   New York
London   Sydney   Tokyo   Toronto

AP PROFESSIONAL

An Imprint of ACADEMIC PRESS, INC.
A Division of HARCOURT BRACE & COMPANY

ORDERS (USA and Canada): 1-800-3131-APP or APP@ACAD.COM
AP Professional Orders: 6277 Sea Harbor Dr., Orlando, FL 32821-9816

Europe/Middle East/Africa: 0-11-44 (0) 181-300-3322
Orders: AP Professional 24-28 Oval Rd., London NW1 7DX

Japan/Korea: 03-3234-3911-5
Orders: Harcourt Brace Japan, Inc., Ichibancho Central Building 22-1, Ichibancho Chiyoda-Ku, Tokyo 102

Australia: 02-517-8999
Orders: Harcourt Brace & Co. Australia, Locked Bag 16, Marrickville, NSW 2204 Australia

Other International: (407) 345-3800
AP Professional Orders: 6277 Sea Harbor Dr., Orlando FL 32821-9816

Editorial: 1300 Boylston St., Chestnut Hill, MA 02167 (617)232-0500

Web: http://www.apnet.com/approfessional

United Kingdom Edition published by
ACADEMIC PRESS LIMITED
24–28 Oval Road, London NW1 7DX

ISBN 0-12-196540-6

Printed in the United States of America
96 97 98 99 IP 9 8 7 6 5 4 3 2 1

CONTENTS

v

Part IV: Mutual Fund Company Web Sites — **163**

Chapter 10: The Big 3—Fidelity, Schwab, and Vanguard — **167**

Chapter 11: No-Load and Other Mutual Fund Sites 205

Chapter 12: Discount Brokers 229

Part I

Introduction

1

Why Invest on the Internet: An Introduction

This book isn't one of those books that tells you how to make lots and lots of money. Nor does it contain a "secret system" for trading mutual funds on the Internet. It does, however, give you a clear overview of the investment and mutual fund resources available on the World Wide Web. And it does tell you which sites and companies to patronize and which to avoid. This advice alone should save you plenty of today's most important resource: time. The book does tell you how to make, and save, money—but only in a most conservative manner.

Until recently, I preferred the world of paper transactions—before I was catapulted into the world of mutual fund Websites and "dollar bytes" by the signing of a book contract. But I've become a believer. Though I can't make you rich (nobody can, except maybe you … or a will executor), I will show you some great ways to use your PC to simplify your personal finances and investment planning. Wait and see. You'll become a believer, too.

As you read this book, you'll discover that I'm far from a fanatic about technology. Although I will passionately urge you to embrace those areas that I feel will make your life easier, I also won't hesitate to direct you to phone or paper alternatives if I feel they have an advantage. Investing is a long-term endeavor; the use of computers requires not less but more vigilance.

Investing on the Internet is the same as investing anywhere, whether over the phone or through the mail. But the Internet is safer, faster, and cheaper. Because of its low costs, efficiency, and most of all its safety, the World Wide Web will be where you make your mutual fund transactions in the future. It's only a matter of time. Already, hundreds of mutual fund companies and millions of investors have left the paper world behind (well, a big part of it, anyway). These online pioneers are requesting stock and fund quotes, reading investment articles and advice, and checking account balances online. Yes, many are even trading online.

All this, and no hackers have ripped off a billion electronic dollars. As a matter of fact, although there have been a few documented cases, incidents of electronic fraud and larceny have been amazingly few. For some reason, consumers demand an extra degree of safety from computer transactions. They don't insist that their phone calls, mail, or other transactions be foolproof, yet they do when they're online. Luckily, the machines are ready to oblige.

Some people do remain hesitant because they're still uncomfortable with the technology. Within the next year, though, you'll see a significant portion of the leading-edge mutual fund companies' trades executed, confirmed, and approved directly over the Internet. By the end of 1997, Internet transactions could even rival 800-number transactions in total volume, given the current growth rates. And yes, it's even safer than any other form of transaction and communication.

A truly electronic trade or communication may be checked, recorded, and reviewed if necessary. Actual thefts on the information superhighway are sparse for a reason; everyone is being watched. Tracing a perpetrator on the Internet is much easier than tracking him or her elsewhere. So, security isn't a reason to hold back, contrary to what the media has implied.

As cyberprophet William Gibson remarked, "The future has already arrived–it's just not evenly distributed yet." Right now, the technologically savvy small investor, for mere pennies, has at his or her disposal market and company information that used to cost professional investors thousands of dollars per month. Even those investors requiring extensive guidance can find it more quickly and more cheaply than they ever could before. Granted, there is still a lot of useless information and self-interested advice on the Web; however, the proliferation of truly helpful, educational, and objective information has made it possible for anyone to become his or her own investment advisor. And people are doing it in record numbers.

There may be too much information on individual stocks available online, but the commentary and advice devoted to mutual funds is more manageable. The major mutual fund company Web sites, in particular, make it silly for anyone with a computer and a modem to overpay for advice. These companies have compiled an extensive array of helpful materials, which alone make the Net worth surfing.

The Web has truly leveled the playing field for the little guy. Costs have been reduced, investment information is instantly updated and disseminated, and the computer plays no favorites—small investors are truly able to attain par with professional investors. Though these developments are still in their early stages, the implications are already clear. The traditional full-service brokerage and financial firms with high fixed-costs will continue to lose market share to the leaner, lower-cost companies.

The bulk of Internet trading will take place through no-load mutual fund groups, or those that charge no sales commissions, like Fidelity Investments and The Vanguard Group. The full-service brokerages, such as Merrill Lynch and Paine Webber, have strong incentives not to trade online because their brokers would be taken out of the commission loop. Even as the spread of toll-free 800 numbers made possible the rapid growth of no-load mutual funds, the World Wide Web revolution is taking us to the next level. Investors are able to seek out their own investment ideas and become their own brokers like never before.

Don't get me wrong—full-service brokers aren't going out of business any time soon. Much of the information and advice on the Web is self-serving, useless, or downright dangerous. There is already too much hype, and expectations are already sky high, but, like it or not, the Internet has become a force in today's financial marketplace.

As thousands of media and financial companies continue to add investment resources, the need for an online investor's guide has grown. The amount of information that has become available, especially within this last year, is enough to keep the average consumer reading for decades. Although you and I can't hope to keep pace with the explosion of news, numbers, and advice, I do believe that this book will serve as an extremely helpful road map to get you started. Anyone, from the novice to the expert computer user, from mutual fund beginner to guru, should benefit from and, I hope, enjoy this book.

Over the last year alone, the number of personal computer owners has grown to almost half of all U.S. households, while the number of mutual fund investors includes well over half of all households. Both groups barely existed a mere 20 years ago, but at their current growth rates it won't be long before every single household owns a PC and invests in at least one mutual fund.

The simultaneous explosion in the populations of these two groups—PC owners and mutual fund investors—is no coincidence. Funds brought professional investment management and service to the masses, while PCs brought computing power to the people. With the meeting of the two, we have new industries, technologies, and products developing at such a rapid rate, you practically need a mainframe computer to keep score.

Luckily, the Internet has made keeping score possible. Now, not only can you go out and get almost any information instantaneously, you can even tell your computer to go out and get the information for you. What six months ago was an overhyped, overpriced way to add pictures to your text has now become an analytical animal. With the latest generation of computer hardware, software, and Internet connections, the individual investor has gained instant access to enough investment information to trade and compete with the best minds on Wall Street.

This book is designed to provide a guide to no-load mutual fund and investment resources on the Internet and major online services. I also hope to give you some very sound investment advice. But, most importantly, I hope to inspire you to use your computer to become your own investment advisor. *Mutual Fund Investing on the Internet* reviews the basics of computers and investing, then evaluates the biggest and most useful World Wide Web sites on the quality of their investment advice and information. This book will give you guidance on trading mutual funds online, and it will show you how to save time and money in your search for investment knowledge.

My personal approach is a blend of frugal, conservative, and contrarian investment philosophies, which should offer a nice contrast to the preponderance of "hypesters" on the Web, those urging you to make a quick and easy buck, usually by buying their stock or the stock of one of their backers. This viewpoint—that self-directed, lower-cost, well-established techniques and principles will serve investors best–will be stressed in the tour of how computers help us invest, make, and save money. However, other investment philosophies will be examined as well for contrast. Mutual fund Web sites will be looked at in-depth, as will companies with resources and investments available on the Web.

I've tried to write this book so that you may find your own way. I recognize that in today's world, only those areas that directly affect you are relevant. So, there are plenty of indexes, lists, and cross-references for those investors who want to read only about specific investment areas. I've taken the view that investors should tame the technology and not let the technology tame them. In other words, when I've come across features and operations where paper or the telephone is still easier than the Internet, I let you know it!

After all, the goal of using the computer is to make your life easier. If it doesn't do that, don't use it.

A Brief History of Computers and Investing

Confusion in choosing where to invest is ubiquitous. As the amount of information and news affecting the investment world has grown, so has the need for sophisticated electronic tools to keep track of it all. Of course, since the dawn of investing, sophisticated market participants have used computing tools to gain an advantage over the competition. Today's worldwide financial system would be helpless without electronic assistants. But how did this relationship develop over the last 20 years?

Certainly, the large investment banks and trading houses, such as Goldman Sachs, Salomon Brothers, and Merrill Lynch, have had mainframe computers and state-of-the-art equipment tracking the markets for them for decades. The nature of finance—where split seconds and accurate data can mean millions—has kept it on the cutting edge of technology. But only since the dawn of the personal computer in the mid-1980s have the tools needed for extensive technical or fundamental research been available to smaller investors.

Beginning in 1985, discount brokers such as Charles Schwab and Quick & Reilly (who remain at the forefront of technology) began offering discounts for customers who used PCs to place orders. While these discounts also applied to their 800 number "tele-broker" services as well, they established a core user community that pushed for enhancements and the availability of more investment information. The PC, and then the spread of online services, fueled these trends.

Things have come a long way. Charles Schwab recently estimated that approximately 30 to 40 percent of investment trades will be transacted over the Internet within the next few years. At present, estimates of the total percentage of Schwab's trades placed via PCs range up to 25 percent. Commenting on why the companies themselves prefer the Internet over proprietary software, Schwab spokesperson Tom Taggart explains, "The Internet is a lot easier for companies to enhance and change."

In all, experts estimate that almost a million electronic brokerage accounts are now open, either directly through the Internet or via proprietary in-house software. This number will only grow in the coming months. Of the estimated total 60 million brokerage accounts and estimated 135 million mutual fund accounts open in the United States, up to half of these should be able to place transactions online by the end of 1997. And while mutual fund investors have traditionally lagged behind individual brokerage account customers (who trade individual stocks) in adapting to new technology, this is beginning to change.

The spread of mutual funds has coincided with the spread of PC use, so investors have come of age familiar with the benefits (and drawbacks) of electronic investing. Figure 1-1 shows the number of mutual fund shareholders plotted against the number of PC users over the last 20 years. As you can see, the growth in each group has been phenomenal over the past 10 years. At these rates of growth, almost every family in the United States will have at least one computer user and one mutual fund within two years (on average).

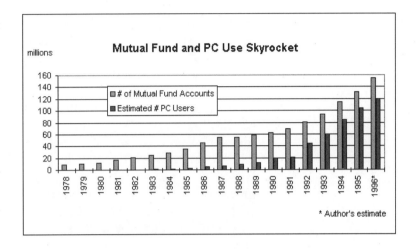

Figure 1-1. The exponential growth in fund PC use parallels fund use.

Source: 1996 *Mutual Fund Fact Book*, Investment Company Institute, Washington, DC.

Using the PC for gathering information and tracking mutual fund investments is a natural fit. Even though volumes have been produced covering either computers or investing, there remains a void between the two subjects. The tremendous growth of the Internet's World Wide Web, in particular, has dramatically increased the availability of market information to the individual investor, while the equally impressive growth of assets invested in no-load mutual fund companies has provided a gigantic target audience. Thus, it is a fortuitous time to take advantage of today's technology.

Investing *with* computers is just now beginning to enter the mainstream, and yet the field has been ill explored. Many books and articles have focused on individual stocks and have missed the greater and safer opportunity in mutual funds.

Unfortunately, as the amount of information on investing has exploded, so has the potential for danger. Most of the investment recommendations in newspapers, magazines, and newsletters are written by self-interested parties. The writer often has investments in either the company or fund group, and the publisher often has advertising relationships with investment companies. Even though it is impossible to avoid all conflicts of interest in investment advice, you should always be aware of the potential for self-interested commentary.

The Explosion of No-Load Funds on the Web

While mutual funds have seen incredible growth in the past 20 years, the biggest gains have come among the no-load funds—those that do not charge a sales commission. The spread of 401(k) plans also has been a major factor in this growth; employers have moved toward giving their workers more autonomy. In the interest of serving this market as well, we will concentrate on the biggest no-load fund groups—Fidelity Investments, The Vanguard Group, and Charles Schwab.

Although I do mention Web sites involving full-service brokerage firms and "load" funds, this group has a much lower profile due to the "do-it-yourself" nature of the Web. Though there are plenty of counterexamples, which we'll visit, you'll probably notice that most of the advertisements on the Web are from these no-load companies. The appealing demographic qualities of Webgoers are not lost on the no-load companies; they're self-starting, wealthier, and younger than the general populace.

The sheer number of mutual funds, however, has made it almost impossible to choose which ones are right for you. The last thing investors need is for the Web to give them even more choices. It doesn't have to be that confusing.

For the gigantic no-load mutual fund companies—Fidelity, Vanguard, and Schwab—the Web represents their dreams come true: no worries about mailing costs, an affluent, self-reliant clientele, and no toll-free phone bills the size of Rhode Island. The Web represents their ultimate sales tool. Thus, it's no surprise that these companies are moving online *en masse*.

Conveniently enough, the only thing these financial power-houses can't provide is specific investment advice and information, so the Web is a natural. The educational areas alone on the major no-load fund company sites have enough information to keep one reading for years. No single investment advisor or source can compete with the quality and comprehensiveness of these.

No-load mutual fund companies jumped onto the Web early, and they're there to stay. They've also moved forcefully onto the online services—America Online, CompuServe, and Prodigy. But the tremendous growth of the Web, in particular, has dramatically increased the availability of all types of market information to the individual investor.

What do computers and mutual funds have to do with each other, you ask? First of all, both have experienced tremendous growth over the past decade. Neither product existed at the turn of the century, and yet these two industries now affect practically everyone on the planet. More personal computers are being sold than television sets in America per year, while the average American household now owns shares in at least one mutual fund. However, both products remain mysterious to the average consumer.

The World Wide Web sites of fund groups—Fidelity, Vanguard, and Schwab, plus the upstart electronic deep-discount brokers—and of news providers and financial institutions are covered in depth. Mutual funds are a good choice because of their inherent advantages over all other investment types—their safety (through diversity), lower costs (through economies of scale), and ease of use.

No-load mutual fund families are the number one investment advice source on the Web. Though they are prohibited from giving specific investment advice, they provide plenty of helpful information. They make it easy for you to be your own investment advisor, attain better performance, and feel more comfortable about your financial situation.

Remember, the goal of this book is to give you the ability to harness the computer in order to simplify your finances, your investing, and your life. To help you avoid information overload, to avoid scam artists, and most of all to save time in entering the world of online investments, this book has been organized so that experienced investors and experienced Internet browsers both may move quickly past any introductory material.

2

Online Services, the Internet, and the World Wide Web

If you're reading this book, chances are you have probably "surfed the Net" at least once. Chances are also strong that if you're not a frequent user, you've probably thought that the Net was oversold, to say the least. However, all the painful waiting while you download will be worth it. As Randall Langdon of Merrill Lynch said at a conference of mutual fund executives, "One of these mornings we'll wake up and the Internet will be a reality." Good morning, Mr. Langdon. The Internet is here, and it's fast becoming the most important financial communications medium in the world.

This chapter will familiarize you with the Internet's World Wide Web, and it will explain some of the reasons for its popularity. Advanced users may want to read through this chapter quickly, but even they should appreciate some of the statistics listings below. I also explore the downside to this new medium, then review a few definitions.

> *The surging popularity of the Internet is the most important single development in the computer industry since the IBM PC was introduced in 1981.... Like the PC, the Internet is a tidal wave. It will wash over the computer industry and many others, drowning those who don't learn to swim in its waves.*
> —Bill Gates in The New York Times, *1996*

The number of users of the Internet and major online services has grown from approximately 10 million in 1993 to almost 50 million today, and these numbers are still soaring at an incredible 100% per year. There are also over 10 million dedicated servers, and that number has been doubling every year since 1988. Even though these statistics may not seem that impressive in absolute terms, should they continue most of the world will be on the Web soon into the Third Millennium.

Originally, even the primarily text-based nature of early Web sites didn't prevent them from becoming popular; but advances in graphics, sounds, and delivery systems are making some sites irresistible. Already, e-mailed video briefings and personalized newspapers are appearing; it's only a matter of time before live video feeds are routine.

Although there is indeed a phenomenal amount of hype surrounding the Web, the rate at which people are "getting online" has not slowed. In fact, the hype appears to be self-fulfilling, as thousands buy multimedia PCs just to see "what's the big deal?"

Since I began learning about the Internet and World Wide Web just a few short years ago, I have read literally thousands of articles just on the somewhat limited topic of investing on the Internet. Had I read all of the articles that mentioned the term "Internet," the total would probably reach the hundreds of thousands. The growth has been truly awesome to behold. It's easy to wonder what all those HTML programmers, Webmasters, and others were doing last year. Working at Starbucks?

Futurist Nicholas Negroponte of the Massachusetts Institute of Technology's Media Lab has predicted one billion Internet users by the year 2000. Current estimates range from under 10 million users to over 20 million in the United States, but whatever the current count, the numbers are increasing at an astonishing rate[1]. Some say the number of Internet users grows by 8% per month! The Internet certainly can't keep growing at that rate forever. But if it keeps growing at anywhere near that pace, the Internet will encompass most of the civilized world in short order. Whether growing exponentially or not, it's clear that there are a tremendous number of Internet users and that the growth is nowhere near abating.

Another estimate comes from MCI Senior Vice President Vinton Cerf (known to some as the father of the Internet due to his relentless proselytizing). He said to *The Wall Street Journal*, "I'm not at all shy about predicting that by 2005, the Internet will be as big as the telephone system is today [approximately 660 million lines installed]." He might have added that it will probably *include* the telephone system, as well.

---

[1] The latest studies range from 9.5 million U.S. Internet users (Find/SVP) to 19 million (Nielsen).

The true promise of the new medium comes from several factors. First, it can do anything that a conventional communications device can do—act as a phone, a fax, or a television—only more cheaply and more quickly. Its multimedia capabilities allow users simultaneous sight and sound. Although all of this hasn't come to pass yet for many consumers, it's only a matter of time and price. Consumers won't even have to wait for cable modems, fiber-optic lines, or other hardware improvements, although these too will come.

Already, the launch of MSNBC—the joint venture of Microsoft Corp. and NBC—has begun the merger of TV and the Internet. "Eventually, technology will permit real-time video and high-fidelity sound," MSNBC says. Even though not exactly "high-fidelity," real-time audio works fine with the current hardware, and video quality is acceptable due to advances in compression technology.

The surging economic strength of the Internet is just beginning to be felt. An AP story quotes Larry Gerbrandt, a media analyst for Paul Kagan Associates: "People are turning off their TV sets and turning on their computer monitors. It's already affecting everything from video rentals to prime-time ratings." And its impact will only increase.

Long-distance companies are seeing a drop in revenues as e-mail spreads. Local companies are seeing a surge in revenues as second phone lines are added, and utilities are having trouble keeping up with the explosion in power usage that the information revolution is driving. Other effects remain to be seen, but it's clear that the new paradigm is causing myriad and unpredictable effects on every industry in the world.

Why the Web?

The biggest advantage the Internet's World Wide Web has over conventional communications media is its versatility. It can be more than an 800 number, better than voice mail, and yet cheaper than both (eventually, anyway). With somewhere in the neighborhood of 100 million "pages" of information, the Web is already by far the largest library in the world. As a matter of fact, it may eliminate the need and enormous expense of libraries everywhere.

You might ask, what benefits does the Web bring to investing? For the investment companies, the advantage is mainly cost-savings. When you're updating your site, it's finished, it's instantaneous, and it only has to be in one place. There have been few studies on cost comparison to date, but once the initial Website cost is absorbed, it's ridiculously cheap to maintain when compared to the same resources previously used to perform a task. One Webmaster updating information full-time could replace an entire department of 800-number service reps or an entire staff of salespeople.

Of course, this advantage has tremendous implications for businesses, some of which may see their traditional functions disappear. Although this business sea change, like any, will certainly cause tremendous pain, dislocation, and turmoil for many workers, the end result will free up huge portions of the workforce for more productive uses. And, more importantly, it will lower the cost of products and services across the board.

Speed and efficiency also make the Internet an attractive alternative avenue for investment companies to conduct their communications. Many companies began this trend through the use of e-mail or groupware like Lotus Notes, but the Internet has made these applications all the more powerful.

Other examples abound. Instead of buying this book, you could conduct a search for the term "mutual fund investing on the Internet" in some of the major search engines. Readers of hard-to-find or out-of-state newspapers or magazines no longer have to embark on hour-long journeys scouring local convenience stores for the last copy. Products may be viewed, compared, and purchased in the time it takes you to warm up your car to go to the store.

Besides convenience, the Internet has made the "real-time economy" a reality, where transactions take place immediately. While some Luddites among you may consider that a bad thing, the rest of the world is rejoicing at their new-found freedom. No longer will your creativity or productivity be stifled because some information source is "closed." The Internet is always open.

Certainly, the Web will have a hard time living up to its billing as the biggest thing since electricity, but it's off to an impressive start. In the investment area alone, there are tens of Internet indexes that track companies that are prominent in the new medium, several "Internet" mutual funds (that either invest in Internet companies or take investments only via the Internet, or both), and hundreds of fund sites on the Internet.

The Downside

Of course, the rapid spread of Webmania has a downside, especially if you're in business or if you're an employee who now has twice as much work due to maintaining a Website. Some executives are ignoring it, some are leaping in with both wallets, and some are frozen in sheer terror at anything with "tech-" in front of it. As the Web revolutionizes how consumers get their information, it is also reshaping practically every industry on the planet. Even though some may not be aware of this yet, those in the computer and media fields are already feeling the impact.

According to Vinton Cerf of MCI, "The explosive growth of the Internet has led to rush-hour traffic conditions for many users." Though MCI and practically everyone else is rushing to add capacity, there remain tremendous delays. Plus, the time wasted by employees surfing the Net alone can probably be measured in the billions of dollars, but this could also be considered as a down payment on future productivity. Of more concern to many is the brutal price competition that the Web encourages.

As news-terminal provider Michael Bloomberg has said, "You can go to the Internet and a million people give you free quotes. Everybody's giving information away. Nobody's made any money yet, other than people like Netscape who sell software to people who think they're going to make money.... I can't say whether anyone's ever going to make any money ... on the Internet." It has become a deadly game of high-tech "chicken," with those who can stand the losses long enough triumphing.

Although useless data, delays and crashes, and other frustrating problems abound, the Web is here to stay. One of the best quotes about the troubles and frustrations experienced in the early days of the Web is from digital publisher Michael Wolff (quoted on Prodigy's Business News). He said, "I'm old enough to remember when you had to shake the television and punch the television and only one person in the family knew how to hold the antenna to get the reception you wanted, and that's really where we are with this medium. We've made tremendous strides in the last two years, but we're not slick yet."

There are also privacy, regulation, and "social stratification" issues that are of concern. We'll discuss some of these in later chapters, but these topics are mainly beyond the scope of this book.

Emerging Standards

The battles over standards in the computer industry fill libraries, and the battles over the Internet are the latest and most important of these conflicts since the introduction of the personal computer in the early 1980s. First, it was IBM versus Apple, then Windows versus OS/2, and now Microsoft Explorer versus Netscape Navigator. (For techies, there's Microsoft's ActiveX standards versus Sun Microsystem's Java applets and Netscape's Corba and ONE, or open network environment, platform—standards for writing Internet software). The winner has not always been the best, or the biggest for that matter.

The new "Netscape model" is for business to give away the product. "It used to be that to make money, you had to keep [a product] proprietary. Now to make money you have to make it a standard…. You have to go to the public domain if you want anything to be popular," says Apple Vice President Larry Tesler. Adds Ted Julian, an analyst at International Data Corporation, "There's this sense of, 'Let's figure out how to make the money later….' They hope that as the Internet tide rises, it will lift up all boats.... There's this sense of a pot of gold at the end of the rainbow—if we take this technology and share it with people, one way or another there's going to be lots of money to be made."

The rapid changes and complexity of the new medium have made proprietary products almost obsolete. Bill Gates says, "The competition is very healthy. We're going to keep each other honest. No one's going to get something that's completely proprietary." It remains to be seen just how long this new paradigm can hold, but for now it's the way.

Just as the battle for PC standards in the eighties resulted in the "Wintel" dynasty—Intel's 386, 486, and now Pentium, semiconductors and Microsoft's Windows operating systems—with a single dominant player in each field, so too will today's battles over the structure and standards of the Internet. The winners will produce the hardware and software for most of the world's computers.

Browser Neutral?

Though many of my screen prints in the book were taken with Netscape's Navigator 3.0, this doesn't mean that I endorse one browser over another. It's just what I happen to use. Most screens will look nearly identical, and each browser has its merits.

Of course, many industry participants are already predicting the downfall of Netscape, due to the aggressive integration of Internet Explorer with Windows that Microsoft is embarking upon. As Adam Schoenfeld of Internet consultant Jupiter Communications says, "It's dangerous to impress Microsoft too much with an innovative application. Ask Lotus 1-2-3." While Netscape is far from doomed, readers whose systems are already loaded with Microsoft's Internet Explorer shouldn't be concerned about not having Netscape.

Microsoft's tremendous advantage lies in its power over Windows 95. With Microsoft Internet Explorer built in to practically every computer shipped today, and the leverage this gives Microsoft in dealing with Internet service providers (ISPs) and online services, it does indeed look perilous for Netscape. Already, Microsoft has announced deals with the biggest players—America Online, AT&T (after Netscape had reached deals with both), and Netcom—to become the browser of choice in exchange for a coveted spot on the Windows 95 desktop (a slot in the *Start* menu).

But don't count Netscape out. It maintains a lead in technology, and it too has plenty of agreements with access and content providers. Perhaps its biggest ace is the cachet it carries with Webmasters, many of whom are independent sorts who dislike Microsoft just because it's so big. Either way you look at it, having two big competitors is always better than one.

Current debates involve ActiveX technology, which is an open set of technology specifications for integrating Internet components. ActiveX is Windows-specific, however, while Netscape's broader set of industry standards, Netscape ONE, can be used on any Internet system. Even though these issues may be of interest only to the true tech-heads among you, everyone will be affected by their outcome. Investors in particular should be aware of these issues because these companies are becoming bellwethers not just for the technology stock sector, but for the entire market.

Of course, new battles are shaping up. One of the biggest should be the PC (or workstations at the high-end) versus the $500 box or terminal. Oracle Systems has been one of the companies pursuing this scenario—one in which consumers could buy a cheap "terminal" that gives them access to the Internet. Many technical issues remain, but one of the most exciting promises of the new medium—the delivery of applications (or applets) over the Internet to your terminal—could well make the PC obsolete. However, this is down the road a bit (the road keeps moving faster, though!).

The last, best hope for keeping Microsoft from controlling the universe now rests with Netscape Corporation. From nowhere, this company, founded by Marc Andreeson and run by James Clarkdale, came to dominate the Internet browser market. They used the "UNIX (operating system) strategy"—give the product away in order to create a standard, then make money by charging later for expert or consulting advice. It worked; Netscape dominated over 90 percent of the market in early 1996.

However, Netscape's lead is being seriously challenged by Microsoft's aggressive push into the market. Microsoft's distribution of Internet Explorer with every copy of Windows makes it the automatic favorite in the coming clash. Netscape is sometimes considered the underdog with an 80 percent market share!

The recent release of Internet Explorer 4.0 has upped the ante; this software has integrated the Windows desktop and the Internet, making it easier to find information on both (and making it appear seamless to the user). This link between browser and operating system (not to mention between applications as well) poses a tremendous quandary for users: Netscape or Microsoft.

The Players

Although the purpose of this book is to help you use your computer to make the investing process simpler and more efficient, some of you may have expected a tome discussing investing *in* the Internet (i.e., investing in the stocks of Internet companies). Here, and later in the investing basics section, I hope to dissuade you from investing in the stocks of these high-fliers.

Even though the investment potential for some of these companies is enormous, so are the risks. Even an investment in a gigantic or super-growth company like IBM or Microsoft could drop severely in value, devastating those investors who are not prepared to wait out any cyclical market moves. Nonetheless, the following chapters refer to some of the newer technology companies so many times that I'd be remiss without at least mentioning the more prominent ones.

Table 2-1 lists the major players in the computer and Internet industries, along with a brief explanation of the industry they're in and the products they produce. Though this list is by no means comprehensive, it will definitely give you a good idea of the types of companies, as well as many of the major players, that are involved with building, maintaining, and populating the Internet.

The Internet-access providers and online service companies are reviewed in further detail in Chapter 7. Also, some of the larger media companies are covered in Chapter 8, while the mutual fund and other financial companies are listed in later chapters. I may have excluded some of the smaller start-up firms (my apologies), but the following does represent the vast majority of the computer players on the Internet.

Table 2-1 Internet Players Index

Hardware Companies

Company	Symbol	Business/Products
Apple Computer	AAPL	Computers
Ascend Communications	ASND	Makes hardware for WANs (wide area networks)

Table 2-1 Continued

Hardware Companies

Company	Symbol	Business/Products
Bay Networks	BAY	Networking: routers, hubs, switches
Cascade Communications	CSCC	Networking
Cisco Systems	CSCO	Networking: routers, hubs, switches
Dell Computer	DELL	PC maker (mail order)
Diana	DNA	Internet switching technology
Digital Equipment	DEC	PCs, workstations, mid-sized, other hardware
Gateway 2000	GATE	PC maker
Hewlett-Packard	HWP	PCs, workstations
Intl. Business Machines	IBM	Mainframes, minis, PCs, software
Intel	INTL	Semiconductors (Pentium, Pentium Pro)
Iomega	IOMG	Disk drives (Zip)
Micron Technology	MU	Semiconductors
Motorola	MOT	Semiconductors, communications technology

Continued

Table 2-1 Internet Players Index Continued

Hardware Companies

Company	Symbol	Business/Products
Seagate	SEG	Disk drives
Shiva	SHVA	Phone systems
3Com	COMS	Networking: routers, hubs, switches
US Robotics	USRX	Modems and telephony products

Communications/Access Providers

Company	Symbol	Business/Products
AT&T	T	Phone, communications, (*WorldNet* Internet service)
America Online	AMER	Online service provider (OSP)
Bolt Beranek & Newman	BBN	Networking; specialized software
CompuServe	CSRV	Online service provider (OSP)
IDT	IDTC	Internet service provider (ISP)
MCI	MCIC	Long distance, other
Netcom On-line	NETC	Internet service provider (ISP)
Prodigy	*	Online service provider (OSP)

Table 2-1 Continued

Communications/Access Providers

Company	Symbol	Business/Products
PSINet	PSIX	Internet service provider (ISP)
Sprint	FON	Long distance, ISP, other telecommunications
UUNet Technologies	UUNT	ISP (bought by MFS Communications)

Software

Company	Symbol	Business/Products
Adobe Systems	ADBE	Graphics (Acrobat, PageMaker, PageMill)
Borland	BORL	Language and compiler programs (Delphi)
CyberCash	CYCH	Online transaction systems
Excite	XCIT	Search engine site
Firefox	FFOX	Communications software
FTP Software	FTPS	File transfer protocol software
Gandalf Technologies	GANDF	Remote access and internetworking software
Gartner Group	GART	Strategic consulting
Global Village	GVIL	Communications software

Continued

Table 2-1 Internet Players Index Continued

Software

Company	Symbol	Business/Products
Harbinger	HRBC	Electronic commerce software
Hummingbird	HUMCF	Networking software
Informix	IFMX	Database
Individual	INDV	Agents; customized news, Freeloader
Lycos	LCOS	Search engine site
Macromedia	MACR	Browser plug-in software; maker of Shockwave
Mecklermedia	MECK	Market research on Internet topics
Microsoft	MSFT	Software (most of it)
Netscape	NSCP	Browser software (Navigator)
Netmanage	NETM	Web software (Websurfer)
Novell	NOVL	Network software (NetWare)
Open Market	OMKT	Information-customizing software (OM-Express)
Open Text	OTEXF	Search and Intranet technologies
Oracle	ORCL	Database; planning $500 "Internet box"
PictureTel	PCTL	Video-conferencing software

Table 2-1 Continued

Software

Company	Symbol	Business/Products
Premenos Technology	PRMO	Software for electronic commerce (Templar)
Proteon	PTON	Network software
Qualcomm	QCOM	Eudora e-mail
Quarterdeck	QDEK	Software for marketing goods on Internet
Santa Cruz Operation	SCOC	Software (including version of UNIX)
Spyglass	SPYG	Browser software
Sun Microsystems	SUNW	Workstations, software (Java)
Sybase	SYBS	Database
Verity	VRTY	Search engines
Vocaltec	VOCLF	Audio and voice communication software
Yahoo	YHOO	Internet directory/search

* Company's stock isn't publicly traded yet.

Source: Jupiter Communications, other.

We will come across scores of other companies from other industries, and several comprehensive lists of company sources online are in the appendixes. Look for investment companies to be listed among their individual categories in future chapters.

3

Terminology, Equipment, and Standards

What we are seeing is not just the birth of a new technology, but the springing into existence of a whole new paradigm of culture and communication. This is because the World Wide Web model makes distributing and accessing any form of digital data easy and inexpensive for anyone— company or consumer—with profound implications for business, culture, and society. Thus, it is no surprise that seemingly 'everyone' is now buying or downloading the latest in Web tools and is madly learning how to build pages, so that they too can join this new electronic world.

—Ian S. Graham, author of HTML Sourcebook.

This chapter is divided into two parts. The first covers definitions of terms used on the World Wide Web (both basic and advanced). This part also tells you what's needed and recommended to take full advantage of the Web's offerings, keeping in mind that these standards are shifting quickly. I try to be hardware, software, and browser "neutral," though I do spell out my personal preferences. Advanced Web surfers may skip these basic technology primers, but they should definitely read the latter half of the chapter.

The second part of Chapter 3 explains what's not covered by the book (and why). Because of the immense size and tremendous resources on the Web, the biggest challenge in writing anything about it is keeping the scope manageable. This chapter ends with an explanation of some of the terminology and ratings systems used once we move into the site reviews in Chapters 7-14.

First, I again, and preemptively, apologize for any outdated information given here. The rapidly changing nature of the industry makes it especially ill suited for books. However, I've done my best to make the descriptions time-insensitive. By the time you finish this book, though, you'll be prepared to identify the biggest and most important companies along the information superhighway. Thus, you'll also be able to choose the best products and services.

Definitions

Though many of you are probably familiar with the following terminology, I'm including it in the interest of completeness. This is by no means an exhaustive list of definitions, but I will point you toward several sources where you can start looking for more information here and in the bibliography. I've split the terms into "Basic" and "Advanced."

Although you don't have to know most of these, they're all nice to know. And, should you run into some technical troubles, you may even need to know them. Either way, you will encounter these terms.

Some Basic Web Terminology

URL—Uniform resource locator, or the naming system used to access the address of WWW sites and resources. The URL may be thought of as the address.

Domain—The home computer's name. For example, in the URL `http://www.strong-funds.com`, strong-funds is the domain name of the server computer.

HTTP—Hyper-text transfer protocol, or the standards used to distribute information ("pages") between computers. You'll know it as the prefix to Web addresses (`http://`).

HTML—Hyper-text markup language. The programming code of choice for Web pages (hypertext documents). It allows forms, images, and links to be created easily and in standard format. You'll probably see the file extension on occasion because all "pages" have this extension. For example, one page of a site might be:

`http:\\www.demo.com\news.html`.

FTP—File transfer protocol. A set of standards for sending files over computers. You'll see some sites give you the option of downloading large files using *ftp*.

ISP—Internet service provider (such as Netcom or GNN); connection to the Internet. (These are opposed to online service providers, like AOL and Prodigy.)

Advanced Web Terminology

CGI—Common gateway interface, or specifications that control access to a server computer.

Java—An object-oriented (the parts are interchangeable) computer language used to design dynamic "applets" that can run on any computer. Both Netscape's Navigator and Microsoft's Explorer are Java-compatible.

ActiveX—Microsoft's "applet-language" and set of standards for program development. ActiveX competes with Java.

Open Doc—A rival standard to ActiveX technology, led by Apple and IBM. Apple's CyberDog is an Internet retrieval program that integrates the Web and the desktop (like Microsoft's Internet Explorer 4.0).

SLIP—Serial line Internet protocol (connection). SLIP and PPP (below) are methods of connecting to the Internet via modem. Thankfully, that's all you need to know.

PPP—Point-to-point protocol. You need a SLIP or PPP connection for Internet access, which service providers and online services give when you dial in.

POP—Point of presence. Local calling connection that links to the Internet. This is the place your ISP dials into.

POP3 Server—Server used for incoming mail. Mail programs need this to retrieve; it's normally the term "popd" in front of your domain name (i.e., popd.prodigy.com)

SMTP Server—Server for outgoing mail. (smtp.prodigy.com).

The Necessary Equipment (Hardware and Software)

You're probably well aware by now that you need a personal computer (preferably with a fast Pentium microchip) with a modem (preferably 28.8kbps or faster), and Internet access in order to visit World Wide Web sites. For the sake of uniformity, we will assume the reader to be using a PC, Windows 95, and Netscape Navigator (3.0+) or Microsoft Internet Explorer (3.0+) browser. Most sites should vary only slightly for other configurations.

Recommended Equipment

I recommend a multimedia PC with CD-ROM, sound card and speakers, and the highest quality monitor you can afford. It should have the following as features:

Pentium or Pentium Pro Processor (the higher the megahertz, the better)
16 megabytes RAM (memory) minimum
1.5 gigabyte hard drive minimum
28.8 kbps modem minimum
Windows 95 or Windows NT operating system
Netscape Navigator 3.0+ or Microsoft Explorer 3.0+

A machine like this will cost anywhere from $2,000 to $4,000, depending on its quality and features. (I recommend the mail order PC companies, like Gateway 2000, but you should buy from the vendor with whom you are most comfortable.)

What's Not Covered in This Book

As I've mentioned, the hardest task on the Internet isn't finding, it's filtering. The amount of information is so enormous that one could spend days searching (as I'm sure you're aware). So, I've made a concerted effort to exclude certain things. While this may disappoint some readers, it had to be done. Below, I explain my reasoning for omitting the following topic areas.

Individual Stocks

In Chapters 4 through 6 I lay out my investment philosophies, but suffice it to say that covering individual stocks would've added another 600 pages to this book. However, a tremendous overlap exists between funds and stocks, so an abundance of information is referenced. Nonetheless, the purpose of buying mutual funds in the first place is to spare you from the extensive research needed to choose individual stocks.

Quotes are discussed throughout, but I concentrate on fund quotes only. Of course, most sites that allow for quotes have both mutual funds and individual securities (i.e., stocks). Several excellent sites are provided. Note: While stock quotes are almost always 20-minute-delayed (it used to be 15 minutes, plus five for delivery, but the delivery has been reduced to zero, so another five-minute delay was added), funds only have one price per day. So, you don't need to keep checking a fund price—it doesn't change until after the market closes (they'll be updated around 6 p.m. EST). I'll return to this topic in Chapter 4.

Technology stocks are also omitted, but as you can guess after reading "The Players" section in Chapter 2, they will be mentioned here and there. As you'll see, however, avoiding information on technology companies in most of the investment areas reviewed is just about impossible.

Software

Here, too, coverage of this field would have made the book too unwieldy. Though I will occasionally mention personal finance programs, like Intuit's Quicken personal finance software, or specialized fund software, like Morningstar's Principia (which ranks and has data on thousands of funds), I don't cover them fully.

I do, however, try to make you aware of the products available from the site-sponsors, in case you'd like to investigate the products yourself. (I also mention programs available from fund companies, if they're offered at the site.)

Foreign Information

Though I do discuss international mutual funds, those funds that invest in Europe, Japan, and other countries, I ignore Canadian and other countries' resources. Investing directly in foreign countries is highly speculative, unless done through a fund company or large organization (or unless you're quite familiar with the territory). There is a tremendous amount of international information on the Internet, but we're going to ignore it.

One thing you'll find when you begin searching out investment data is that Canadian investors have a strong presence on the Web. Beware! Canadian stock promoters are notorious for hyping gold, natural resource, and "penny" stocks—all highly speculative investments. For this reason, and because U.S. investors can't invest in Canadian funds anyway, anything with "Canada" anywhere near it is ignored.

Newsgroups and Bulletin Board Services

I will mention related newsgroups and bulletin board services (BBSs) throughout the book, but overall I downplay them. Certainly, there are some useful and interesting boards, but in most cases the information is downright dangerous. False stories abound, and brokers have taken to these areas like flies on rotting garbage. Do not believe everything you read.

Although this cautionary note applies to almost anything on the Web, even on official sites (which can have outdated or incorrect information), the danger of fraud here is tremendous. I avoid investment newsgroups in particular and downplay any bulletin boards. (Occasionally, I do review so-called "chats" with experts.)

Notes on Standards

Below, I explain some of the setup and conventions of *Mutual Fund Investing on the Internet*. First, once we move into the Website coverage in Chapter 7, you'll see several types of boxes and sidebars; these start in earnest with the actual fund sites covered in Chapter 10. All times noted in this book are in Eastern Standard time (EST), but readers should be aware of the growing preponderance of "Seattle time" on the Web.

Icons

In this book, I use various symbols to describe and mark Websites. The following are some examples.

✳ Website Symbol

This symbol connotes an individual Website. These are the major sites covered in the book. While I do list some other addresses in passing, if it has a Z, I spend some time with the area. Along with the Website's title will be its address (URL):

```
http://www.ibcdata.com
```

I omit the `http://` for brevity, but it is implied. (If there's no www, it's assumed to be missing.) Subsections of a site are then indicated by the slash "/" followed by something. For example, the Money section of USA Today's site is located at:

www.usatoday.com/money (the http:// is implied).

📖 Content Rating Symbol

For each site reviewed, I rate it on three criteria—content, or the amount and quality of information available; appearance, or the look and ease of access to essential information; and overall, which combines the two, but which also considers everything else about the site. These factors are all rated on a scale of 1 to 5, with 5 the highest and 1 the lowest. Not every site is rated, but all of the mutual fund sites and most of the main investment sites are.

☺ Appearance Rating Symbol

This rating has an eye toward usefulness. If it's pretty but takes an hour to load, a site's appearance rating won't be the best. And, because the actual sites will probably have changed the week after this book was sent to the printers, rating a site's looks alone wouldn't do much good. However, the organization and layout should remain steady. Thus, this rating incorporates functionality as well as features.

👍 Overall Rating Symbol

Five "thumbs-ups" is the highest rating, which is given to only those sites that offer excellent information and are entertaining and easy to access. I attempt to spread out the ratings, but those with the lowest—only one "thumbs-up" are omitted in many cases.

⊕ Time You Should Spend Symbol

A rating of 5 means to investigate the whole site, while a 1 wouldn't even be worth visiting. (There aren't many 1's included, for obvious reasons.) This is a general guideline, and it will be explained within the text accompanying many sites. I try to give both a length and frequency guide—for example, telling you to spend 10 minutes or so at a site and to check back weekly.

Other Areas

You'll notice selected commentary for certain groupings of sites. Some examples follow:

Don't Miss Features: This lists the number one thing about each site that makes it stand out or that offers an excellent quick stop for browsers.

In Their Own Words: Occasionally, I'll use direct quotes from Webmasters, public relations personnel, or the site itself in describing some features or plans.

How To Get There: These boxes give specific instructions on how to navigate to a certain area of a site.

quick.def(s): These are brief definitions of terminology, set off so that they may be bypassed by more experienced readers.

Disclaimers

There is a difficulty in writing any book that deals with topics like the Internet. Do you concentrate on content, or do you rush it out so that the subject matter is fresh? While I believe I've reached a nice compromise with *Mutual Fund Investing on the Internet*, there will, of course, be outdated facts, errors, and omissions. I hope to avoid many of these by including an appendix with instructions on how to reach my up-to-the-minute URL list. But I apologize preemptively for any such problems.

Note that the views expressed in this book are solely my own and have not been approved or endorsed by any organization, including my current employer, IBC Financial Data.

Part II

Investing Basics and Strategies

4

A Brief Overview of Investing

Chapters 4, 5, and 6 cover the basics of investing. Before we proceed into the online world, I want to give a quick overview of the topics of *investing*, *mutual funds*, and *portfolio management*. While you may be familiar with these areas, my approach should, at the very least, offer some unique perspectives. You'll probably want to read these chapters even if you're a professional investor. But if you're anxious to get started, feel free to move straight into Part III.

Part II is partly a definition of terminology and partly a collection of investment advice. It's primary purpose is to exhort you to get moving on your own investment plan. The amount of investment advice on the Internet is enough to overwhelm even the most sophisticated market participants. It is essential that you have a good idea of what types of things you are looking for. As a matter of fact, one of the most important functions of this section is to tell you what kind of information you *don't* need. This should save you plenty of time once we begin surfing in Chapter 7.

Even though I do discuss individual stocks here, again the emphasis is on mutual funds. Often the terms "fund" and "stock" are used interchangeably, but there are important differences. Though the growth of lower-commission discount brokers has narrowed the cost gap between stocks and funds somewhat, funds still have the advantage here. They offer more diversity, liquidity, and predictability than stocks. Thus, though any discussion of investments must involve stocks, I set out the basic premise that no-load, low-cost mutual funds are the primary vehicles individuals should use for their investments.

Unless you've got an extensive portfolio (or a complicated personal situation), you really don't need to spend money for a stockbroker. You probably also don't need any other types of financial advisors any longer—from personal money managers to investment newsletters. Now that the Internet has made so much educational material available, it's become easier than ever to run your own portfolio. (More on this topic will be covered in Chapter 6.)

Understanding basic investment concepts and philosophies is central to finding the best and most fitting services, advice, and information. My rapid-fire tutorial should save you from losing money. After reading this, you'll be able to spot investment advice that falls outside the norm. Very few educational investments pay for themselves as quickly as those involving your finances.

In decades past most people could live in blissful ignorance while employers handled their pensions and brokers handled their stocks, but this is no longer the case. The relentless forces of competition are pushing every worker to be his or her own investment manager, both at work and at home. At the same time, the deterioration of personal service relationships has increased the opportunity for deception; people no longer know their banker or broker. I intend to show how to approach both of these dilemmas by sticking with the large, reputable companies of the no-load mutual fund industry.

While the spread of information and technology has opened up tremendous opportunities to the individual, it has also opened the door to bad advice, losses, and fraud. "Investor beware" is my first word of advice; nowhere is this more important than in the online world. By familiarizing yourself with markets, mutual funds, and the economy, you will be better prepared to understand and utilize the Web sites and information centers covered later in the book. And as mentioned, I also hope to show you why not to bother with much of the information out there—just because it's in electronic form doesn't necessarily make the information any better.

Legend has it that when he was asked what the Seven Wonders of the Ancient World were, Baron Rothschild replied, "I surely know not ... but the eighth must be compound interest." This is the miracle of investing: You can earn a single dollar that may then go on to earn itself back many times over. Money invested even in small sums, and at small rates of return, can grow into awesome fortunes ... if given enough time. Of course, the higher the rate of return and the larger the initial investment, the faster the exponential compounding of growth will kick in. At 7 percent interest, a $1,000 investment will grow into $3,870 in 20 years.

But at 14 percent per year, it will grow into $13,740—more than three-and-a-half times as much!

Although there are thousands of books written on the subject, investing remains one of the most misunderstood and feared topics around. If I accomplish anything in this work, it will be to remove at least some of the apprehension that people have about putting their money into stock, bond, and other, more esoteric, mutual funds. In particular, a number of computer-savvy people are just now becoming familiar with the field of investments; they are one of my primary audiences here. These investors have the advantage of the "pioneer" spirit, unafraid of entering new territory. They also have the advantage of having money to invest.

Investing means a lot of things to a lot of people, but its most common usage refers to the buying and selling of stocks (an ownership stake in a business), bonds (the debt of a business), and mutual funds. Yes, many other types of assets are available, such as real estate, limited partnerships, collectibles, and more, but we'll start with just the instruments above. My goal is the same as economist Herbert Mayo's in his classic introductory work, *Investments*: "While this textbook cannot show you a shortcut to financial wealth, it can reduce your chances of making uninformed investment decisions.[1]"

Chapter 5 will discuss in depth why I'm concentrating so heavily on mutual funds (and why they're a perfect fit for the Internet). But for now suffice it to say that this is probably where bank robber Willie Sutton would be looking for the loot today (it's where the money is!). The popularity of stock, bond, and money market (cash) mutual funds has skyrocketed in the last decade, growing into more than $3 trillion in assets ... and still counting.

---

[1] "Investments, An Introduction," Mayo, Herbert, The Dryden Press, 1993.

A mutual fund is merely a conduit; a collection of other investments, such as stocks, bonds, or money market instruments. As mentioned, stock mutual funds, which are by far the most widely discussed type of fund, may be considered the same thing as individual stocks (albeit larger and more conservative). Here, and on the Internet, when you hear "stocks," think "stock funds."

A lot of people like to say about the stock market, "It's just like gambling." What these investors fail to see, however, is that in the stock market "casino," there's a payoff of over $1.12 paid out for every $1 bet (12 percent is the average annualized historical return for stocks). Certainly there is risk, but, as you've probably heard a hundred times from the market pundits, *the higher the risk, the higher the return.*

This is the first and perhaps most important lesson of investing. It's a corollary of the "there's no free lunch" theorem. No matter how many times someone says that something is absolutely, positively safe, if it returns more than the market in general does, it's riskier than the market. This is always the case—period. (*Return* is the total gain from an investment—dividends plus any capital gains.)

Though there are risks in everything, some investments *are* guaranteed, such as U.S. Treasury bonds or bank certificates of deposit (CDs). Even these investments, though, could "lose" money in certain situations (if the CD must be sold with an early withdrawal penalty, for example, or if the T-Bond must be liquidated after the principal, or the initial investment, has fallen temporarily in value).

But these government-guaranteed investments give us a starting point—and a default rate of return—from which to measure all other investments. Beginning with the safest of investments, the Treasury Bill (which has a maturity, or due date, of three months, six months, or one year), we can evaluate the risk and possible return of all other financial instruments. Like a bank account, which is also guaranteed by the government, these returns are the absolute floor that all other investments must beat. Why would anyone invest in anything returning less than T-bills or CDs?

The Reasons for Investing

The immediate goal of investing is to make money, of course. But, as I said, anyone can make money. Just buy a CD (not the disc) or a Treasury bond—they're the closest thing to a sure thing that there is in this world. If you hold these instruments until maturity, you'll make exactly how much they said you would. The real challenge, of course, is to be making *more* money. Or at least more money than a savings account, than the cost of living (the rate of inflation), than your neighbor, and so on. Other than making a lot of money, though, the goals of investing are legion—a college education, a house, or, the most common reason, a secure retirement.

The key to successful investing isn't earning the highest return; it's earning a good return *given your objectives and risk tolerance*. Someone planning on using the money to buy a house in a year shouldn't be proud of a 30 percent return in the stock market; he or she should be reprimanded for being invested there in the first place! After all, any drop in the market could have cost him or her the house. Determining what the money is for is the essential first step in deciding how to invest it.

Saving consistently is the safest and easiest way of accomplishing any financial goal (next to inheritance), but it can often be the hardest. While most people would prefer to save some money, and then have that money earn breathtaking returns, it doesn't work this way in the real world—most of the time anyway. Getting together the several thousand dollars that an initial investment program will take can often be difficult. Some investors must start with any available options at work, or with an individual retirement account (IRA). *Tax-sheltered* retirement savings are far and away the best kind, no matter what asset class (i.e., stocks, bonds, or cash) they're invested in.

"Qualified" plans, that is, tax-sheltered retirement savings plans, start out with a huge advantage due to their tax-sheltered status—taxes aren't due until you begin withdrawing the money at retirement. Every investor should look here first, then worry about savings in a regular taxable account. Determine how much income you can afford to put away each month or each paycheck, and invest it for the long term. Automatic deductions from payroll or checking accounts are excellent ways of doing this, but writing out the check, or e-mailing it, will get you the same results.

The biggest advantage of tax-sheltered retirement investing comes from time, and the next biggest comes from discipline. The longer money has to compound, even if it is compounding at lower rates of return, the larger its advantage becomes. And, when you're automatically investing each month without thinking about it, you're forced to buy even when you might not otherwise. These bleak periods are often precisely the time to buy. I return to the concept of investing each month, dollar-cost averaging, in Chapter 6.

Figure 4-1 illustrates this advantage—the longer an investment is left to compound, the more impact the secret ingredient of growth, the "interest on the interest," has on the principal. This is especially true with more aggressive investment options, like stocks or stock mutual funds. Witness the monstrous gains of the Vanguard Index 500 Fund since inception. This fund, the bogeyman of mutual fund managers, mirrors the Standard & Poor's 500 Index, the most widely used "stock market barometer." I'll talk more about this fund, and about indexes in general, later in the book.

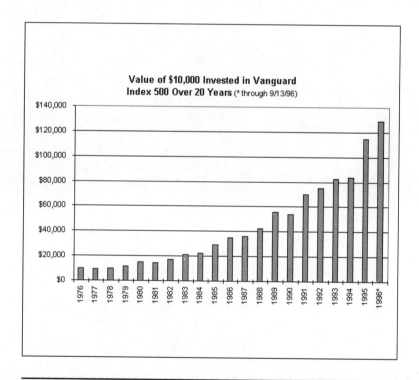

Figure 4-1. Returns like this are why people invest in the first place!

This chart shows that $10,000 invested in the Vanguard Index 500 (an "average" stock mutual fund) at its inception grew more than 10 times over in less than 20 years ($128,883 through Sept. 13, 1996). This assumes that dividends and capital gains were reinvested in additional shares.

Although this clearly demonstrates the allure of stock fund investing, I've included the annual return data below in order to illustrate some of the dangers as well. Though some losses, such as 1977's 7.8 percent drop, may seem small to some, the time period shown began just after a fierce bear market in 1973-74. This downturn lopped off almost 50 percent of investors' principal (this occurred just prior to the period covered by the chart in Figure 4.1). Notice also that 1995's returns were the best since the fund's inception. A word of caution: Investors shouldn't dive into stocks expecting to gain over 30 percent a year—we'll be lucky to see another year like that within the next two decades. Nonetheless, these numbers are meant to inspire you to consider stock mutual fund investing.

Table 4-1 Vanguard Index 500 Fund's Returns Since Inception

Year 1976(yrend)	TOTAL $10,000	Annual Returns	Year	TOTAL	Annual Returns
1977	$9,216	–7.84%	1987	$36,409	4.70%
1978	$9,757	5.87%	1988	$42,314	16.22%
1979	$11,518	18.05%	1989	$55,584	31.36%
1980	$15,195	31.92%	1990	$53,733	–3.33%
1981	$14,403	–5.21%	1991	$69,971	30.22%

Continued

Table 4-1 Vanguard Index 500 Fund's Returns Since Inception
Continued

Year 1976(yrend)	TOTAL $10,000	Annual Returns	Year	TOTAL	Annual Returns
1982	$17,423	20.97%	1992	$75,163	7.42%
1983	$21,133	21.29%	1993	$82,597	9.89%
1984	$22,445	6.21%	1994	$83,571	1.18%
1985	$29,455	31.23%	1995	$114,869	37.45%
1986	$34,774	18.06%	1996*	$128,883	12.20%
20-year Average:		14.40%		* through 9/13/96.	

Before moving on, I want to make just a few brief comments about *saving* in general. Saving money these days is so hard that you owe yourself careful mutual fund selection. Only consider stock funds or aggressive investments if the money is earmarked for long-term investing and isn't needed for two or three years, minimum. Shorter-term, liquid assets, like cash or money market funds, should be used for any savings that might be needed in the near future. Every investor must, of course, consider his or her own situation, but I cannot overstate the importance of a disciplined savings programs.

Remember that even if you lose some money on an investment, if it was money that you would have spent anyway, you're still ahead. So, *any* investment is better than no investment. Next, no one else can tell *you* how to save. Whatever works for you, do it.

Some people need the discipline of monthly withdrawals into savings bonds or mutual funds, while some would prefer to wait for a lump-sum tax refund or year-end bonus to invest. Most of us don't have the luxury of an inheritance or large gift to get started, but even the small investor now has access to much of the same information and professional management (via mutual funds) that was once available to only the most sophisticated professionals. So, though it still helps, it doesn't take a ton of money to make money anymore.

Everyone's Doing It: Investing in the '90s

These days, more and more companies have 401(k) or other "defined contribution" plans—plans that depend on how much employees contribute and earn, not on how generous the company is or how long the employee lives. If you haven't encountered the 401(k) yet, you probably will. The drive to reduce potential corporate liabilities, coupled with the extreme costs involved in administering and insuring traditional pension plans, has made the "pension" of yesteryear a dinosaur.

One of the results of this trend is that, more and more, every worker is being forced (or given the opportunity, depending on how you look at it) to become his or her own investment manager with retirement savings. Like it or not, most of us have little choice but to learn about investing. I think that with the strategies you'll encounter here, and the advice and information to be found on the Internet, you'll learn to like it. After all, making money can be fun!

Much emphasis is placed on the 401(k) plan, as well as on IRAs, Keogh plans and other self-directed, tax-sheltered options, which may invest in mutual funds. This fund information should also be useful for any type of account, so those investors with regular taxable accounts won't feel left out. A secondary goal of mine is to point out the different tactics and types of funds that are most appropriate for each type of investment (taxable versus tax-deferred/retirement). Normally, more aggressive investments should be held in tax-deferred accounts so that these gains may avoid taxation.

The 401(k) plan, or Keogh plan if you're self-employed, is practically free money from Uncle Sam, due to its tax-sheltered nature. If you have the opportunity to invest in one (especially if there's an employer match), take advantage of it. Unless you are going to retire soon and will need the income, put most or all of your contributions into the purest growth vehicle, stock funds, that you can. Though many of these plans have very limited investment options, they all should have at least one stock fund, such as Fidelity Magellan or Vanguard Windsor II. Studies have shown that over the long term, the type of asset class you're in (stocks versus bonds versus cash) determines over 90 percent of your total return. Diversify, but put the bulk of your assets into the broadest stock fund available.

One thing to be wary of is investing in the stock of your own company. Be especially careful here. You could end up losing your pension along with your job should the company go down. However, if you're confident in the company's future, and especially if you can buy the stock at a discount, it probably wouldn't hurt to allocate a fraction (maybe 10 percent, or 20 percent if you're very aggressive) here.

You should also look into IRAs. For those already covered under 401(k) or other retirement plans, they're non-deductible for most, but these still are worth investing in (the earnings compound without being taxed until retirement). Those of you not covered may fund fully deductible IRAs, which can remove up to $2,000 of your income from the taxation rolls.

Your Three Choices: Stocks, Bonds, or Cash

Why stocks? Certainly, if you've made it this far into Part II, you've heard that stocks are the place to be for long-term investors. While I'm not going to argue otherwise, I will warn investors that there is no guarantee this will be the case in the future. *Any long-term investor's primary assets should be invested in stocks, but bonds and cash should be included in every portfolio as well.* This is following the "many eggs *and* many baskets" rule—protect thy nest egg!

Figure 4.2 shows the advantage of stocks over bonds or cash (historically, at least). This chart represents the average annualized returns for four mutual funds—Vanguard Extended Market Index, Index 500, Bond Market Index, and Prime Portfolio Money Market. These funds represent excellent proxies for their respective indexes and fund groups.

Clearly stocks, especially smaller stocks, have had the upper hand for the bulk of this century, but don't forget the risks or volatility. Should you be forced to sell into a down market, you could possibly take dramatic losses. I would not advise putting all of your money into small company stocks tomorrow; you never know when you might be forced to sell. At the same time, you do want some exposure to small companies to spice up your returns a little bit.

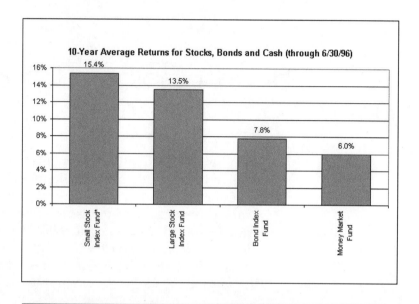

Figure 4-2. Returns for the three major asset classes over the past 10 years.

(Source: Vanguard Group).

Interest Rates and the Economy

Clearly, any discussion of the economy and interest rates that's not an entire textbook must be overly simplistic. I still wanted to mention these areas quickly because practically every market summary or commentary refers to, at least, these areas. While there is no shortcut to understanding these areas, once you've leapt into the investment world you should gradually be able to master the significance of the two topics.

If you've invested before, you know that interest rates, or borrowing costs, often are the single biggest influence on all investments. They affect every debtor and lender on the planet. Rates shift and move as one huge, layered structure 24 hours a day. Stocks certainly react to movements in short- or long-term rates, but bonds are directly affected. Bond prices move inversely with yields—as interest rates rise, bonds fall, and vice versa.

Interest rates influence the economy by making borrowing costs more or less expensive. Because rates (which are equivalent to yields) also compete with stocks for investors' attention, when they rise stocks suffer. Stocks have to become even more attractive to compete as an alternative investment. For example, if rates move up sharply, an investor can earn, say, 8 percent interest on a bond instead of 7 percent. He or she is going to be more tempted by the 8 percent bond investment than previously, which causes stocks to fall as money flows into bonds.

Though there are hundreds of different types of interest rates per se, they all are affected by two things: the demand for money and the actions of the Federal Reserve (the Fed). The Fed sets short-term interest rates, such as the discount rate (what it costs banks to borrow overnight from the Fed) and the more important Federal funds rate (what banks charge each other for overnight loans).

The Fed will increase or decrease rates depending on its outlook for the economy. If it fears an overheating economy and the rise of inflation, it will attempt to slow growth by raising rates and thereby increasing borrowing costs. If the economy is sluggish or in recession, the Fed will cut rates to spur growth. Whenever you hear that the Fed has raised or lowered rates, the short-term rates, Fed funds and discount, are the measures being referred to.

On the other hand, longer-term interest rates, like the 30-year Treasury bond yield, corporate bond yields, or fixed mortgage rates, are set solely by the marketplace (set collectively by the massive government, mortgage, and corporate bond markets). Another widely discussed rate is the prime rate, which is the rate the largest commercial banks charge their most credit-worthy customers. No matter which rate anyone's referring to, though, all are basically the same thing—how much it costs to borrow money.

One of the biggest obstacles to many people's understanding of investing is the role that the economy plays. While it's also beyond my mission here to fully define and describe this beast, I'll give it a mercifully quick shot. The economy is the collective total of cash transactions—measuring the total of the goods and services produced—made in a certain period; its effect on investments stems from its link to interest rates.

When the economy, measured by the gross domestic product (GDP), is expanding, there is upward pressure on interest rates via loan demand (and other demands for money). As more goods and income are made, people feel more confident about borrowing. Conversely, when the economy is contracting, or entering a recession, the demand for money falls, easing pressure on interest rates.

This fact is why so much attention is paid in the financial press to the release of every little economic statistic. If you've ever cursed the release of some data, such as the index of leading economic indicators or capacity utilization, because it triggered a market sell-off, you know what I mean. The financial markets watch every number and blip in economic activity for a hint as to whether the economy is accelerating or decelerating, and at what rate. (Chapter 14 shows where this data may be found on the Web.)

To illustrate, Figure 4-3 shows the quarterly changes in the gross domestic product of the United States since 1987. It is important for investors to know what phase of economic expansion or contraction we are in—whether the economy is growing or contracting. Because certain assets perform better in certain environments (or have historically, at least), investors will want to plan their actions accordingly.

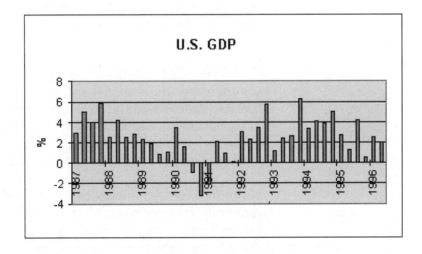

Figure 4-3. A look at gross domestic product (GDP) growth.

(Source: Commerce Department).

This chart clearly shows that the current economic expansion is getting long in the tooth. In this case, as in 1990, you would want to proceed with caution, perhaps by reducing stock exposure in favor of bonds or cash. Though the markets often precede economic activity, it still is wise to be aware of whether growth is accelerating or decelerating. In general, a slowing economy favors bonds, and a speeding one stocks.

During the past decade, stocks have done fabulously, as they normally do during stable growth periods. Bonds have also done spectacularly, which they tend to do during low inflationary periods and recessions, but commodities (which love inflation) have suffered. Commodities investments, like gold, oil, and grains (or the stocks of companies that deal in these materials) benefit from inflation, which is often caused by fast growth. The past decade, however, has been that of the "Goldilocks economic growth"—not too fast, not too slow, but *just* right. While some signs of commodity prices increasing have been spotted, the big inflation warning, rising wages, has yet to appear.

Certain economic data and measurements are taken more seriously by the financial markets than others, but each has its uses. For example, monthly payroll employment data, which measures the number of jobs, is scrutinized intensely because it is a key component of economic growth. This statistic is released simultaneously with the unemployment rate, which is far less important (but is easier for the news media to report). The index of leading economic indicators hints at future direction; CPI (consumer price index), an inflation barometer, reports on durable goods orders and indicates how the manufacturing sector is doing.

All of these measurements are useful and interesting numbers, of which investors should be aware. But investors shouldn't hinge their actions on these statistics. Long-term, conservative investors should focus their energies elsewhere. We'll encounter some of these numbers again in Chapter 14.

Quotations
and Market Terminology

Here is a quick overview of several mutual fund and stock terms used both in newspaper listings and in other contexts. Much of the following jargon is also being used on the Web, but sometimes in a slightly different format. Stock and fund quotes have become one of the most popular items requested on the Internet, but many users are still baffled by some of the symbols and terminology. While I advise against checking quotes too often (it only increases the chance that you'll make a wrong trade), it is useful to check in on your investments periodically.

This overview will also be good for those of you who still fear opening the business section of the newspaper. Both papers and online quote servers usually list stocks from the three big exchanges: the New York Stock Exchange (NYSE Composite or the "Big Board"), the American Stock Exchange (AMEX), and the National Association of Securities Dealer's automated quotations (NASDAQ) or over-the-counter (OTC) market. Also included are mutual funds, and sometimes individual bonds and other investments. If an investment isn't listed in the newspaper or online somewhere, it's probably very small and very dangerous—don't buy it!

One big difference between stock and mutual fund listings is the fund's NAV, or net asset value. This is the equivalent of a stock's price, and it is what you'll pay for each *share* of the listed fund. Also, because funds have only one price (NAV) per day, there will be no daily high or low price—you will have the closing price, which will be the next day's NAV.

While some papers list only the price and perhaps the change from the day before, publications such as *The Wall Street Journal*, *New York Times*, and *Barron's* will have more extensive data. Here is a sample fund listing:

Name	Symbol	NAV	Net Change	YTD Return
Fidelity Magellan	FMAGX	$75.78	+0.07	+4.2%

The name in the listings is often an abbreviation for the official fund (or company) name whenever the full one won't fit (such as *Magln* for Magellan). However, the listings are usually alphabetized according to the fund's full name, so keep this in mind when searching a paper or list with abbreviations. The following terms are normally used for mutual funds, but many apply to stocks as well.

The symbol often isn't listed in newspapers, but it is still being used online, primarily in quote searches. A five-letter symbol normally means a fund (especially if there's an X at the end), or a very small stock (most stocks have three- or four-letter symbols). NAV is the previous day's closing price (net asset values are normally set after the market closes at 4:00 p.m. EST). Net change is the change in price from the previous day's trading, while year-to-date (YTD) return, which has recently become somewhat of a performance benchmark in newspapers, includes the NAV change plus reinvested dividends and capital gain distributions.

Different media will have different formats, but the example above should be helpful. Many search programs use either company abbreviations or full names now, so symbols aren't as important as they once were. Footnotes denoting distributions or fees will vary, so read each table's legend for details.

Common Wisdom on Wall Street

I want to finish my investing introduction with several "Wall Street maxims." These are rules of thumb, common wisdom, or other pithy expressions for investors that you'll most likely come across. I disagree with some of these, and many are downright deceptive, but you'll probably encounter variations of these themes once we begin investigating the Websites. So I wanted to familiarize you. I'll start with the most famous, and the least helpful.

1. Buy low, sell high.

   If only it were that easy! Of course, for prices, low and high are relative terms. The hard part is deciding what's low (on Wall Street, zero is low). Please ignore this saying. I've found a safer corollary in the motto of: "Buy low, buy lower" and the converse, "Sell high, sell higher." (Double-check your reasoning first, though!) Once you've done your research and decided you like a stock or mutual fund, be sure to allow yourself the flexibility to buy even more of it should it go down even further.

2. Don't fight the Fed. Don't fight the tape.

   These are two market favorites. What they are referring to is this: Don't bet against the interest rate trend and don't bet against the market's current momentum, respectively. Everyone who trades stocks has heard these clichés, which is always bad news for a market theory. When the Federal

Reserve is easing (lowering interest rates), expect stock prices to go up—most of the time. The tape refers to the ticker tape (as seen at the bottom of the screen on CNBC), which means that when stock prices are going up, they'll probably continue doing so, and ditto when they're going down.

The problem here, and with all "momentum-style" or trend-following investing techniques, is that once stocks start moving up or down, you've already missed a significant portion of the move. It may look good in the studies, but the market changes directions often. And blindly following any "system"—to jump into the market because rates are declining, for example—is asking for trouble. But be aware of the current rate and market directions at all times. They are very important.

3. Ride the winners; sell the losers.

This one's my personal favorite, but it's awfully hard to follow. It's true that stocks and funds that have done well usually continue to do so, but no strategy is foolproof. The importance of this phrase is to remind you that your first instinct—to sell once you've made a little gain or buy more of a stock once it's gone down—may be wrong. The biggest advantage is that by not selling winners you postpone taxes. There's nothing like having that one investment just grow and grow.

4. Buy on the rumor; sell on the news.

In other words, once the news is out, it's too late. You want to invest before the actual news, not after. Of course, the hard part is figuring out which rumors are true, which is why I advise against trading on rumors *or* on the news. Previously, this saying had been a trader's credo, but now smaller investors are beginning to move in and out of the market rapidly. You shouldn't buy any fund (or stock, for that matter) on a rumor, especially since the Internet now allows unscrupulous operators to spread false or deceptive news instantly.

5. The suggested stock percentage should be 100 minus your age.

Percent allocated to stock = (100 – age)

This is a nice guide for determining the amount of assets an investor should have allocated to stock funds or individual stocks (with the remainder allocated to bonds or cash). For example, someone who is 30 years old should allocate 70 percent (100 – 30) of his or her investments to stock funds, while a 70-year old should have 30 percent (100 – 70) invested in stocks. While many financial planners and writers suggest that this is too low and too restrictive, I believe that it still represents very sound advice.

We'll discuss the concept of asset allocation and recommended percentages for each asset class in greater detail in Chapter 6. None of these sayings, or any other rule, is foolproof. (I know, I've said that already, but it's important!) The more common wisdom you understand, the better able you are to take advantage of new wisdom being formed.

5

Why Mutual Funds?

Mutual funds have taken America by storm. Like the growth in the number of personal computers, which began slowly but became a torrent, the spread of mutual funds has been amazing. Five years ago you didn't know they existed; two years ago you didn't have to pay attention. Now, they're unavoidable. Most people used to let employers handle their pensions, let banks handle their savings, and let stockbrokers buy an individual stock for them here and there. But they're now investing this money on their own, in stock, bond, or money market funds, or in various combinations of these. More than 30 million U.S.

households now own mutual funds, and the number is growing daily[1].

For most investors, individual stocks have proven just too volatile, though you might not know it from the gains of 1995 and early 1996. Buying individual stocks has become overly expensive, except for the largest investors, and even they seem to prefer funds these days. Investors finally got tired of their brokers placing commissions before perfor- mance and suggesting riskier-than-appropriate stocks. Funds have become the investment vehicle of choice for Americans because of their convenience, performance, liq- uidity, and low cost.

While mutual funds were introduced to the United States in 1924 (Scudder of Boston had the first), their recent exponen- tial growth has been fueled by no-load mutual funds in par- ticular. Load funds, or those sold with a sales charge, awakened people to the idea of mutual funds, but the fund broker's interest was not aligned with the client's. Once their investments were freed of fees, loads, and charges, which in the past had eaten up anywhere from 3 percent to 10 percent of capital, mutual funds began to really get noticed.

Figure 5-1 tells the story. It shows the growth of funds assets, dividing them into three classes—stock funds, bond (and income) funds, and money market funds (both taxable and tax-free). The past 50 years have seen fund assets increase almost 3,000 percent—from $1 billion in 1945 to more than $2.8 trillion at the end of 1995. Assets have since surpassed the $3 trillion mark (in the spring of 1996) and show no signs of stopping.

---

[1] *1996 Mutual Fund Fact Book*, Investment Company Institute, Washington, DC.

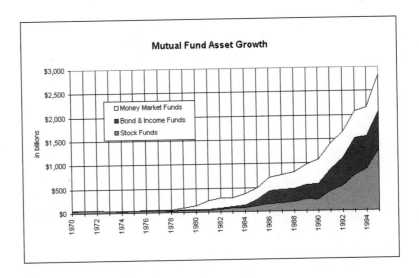

Figure 5-1. Fund assets just keep going and ...

(Source: *1996 Mutual Fund Fact Book,* Investment Company Institute, Washington, DC.).

Mutual funds benefit from tremendous economies of scale by pooling assets. While the small investor buying a couple hundred shares of IBM will pay a couple of percentage points in commissions to his or her broker, mutual funds pay only a fraction of a percent because of the massive orders they place. Just as the mutual fund industry has been faster and more efficient than the banking industry due to its lack of expensive "brick-and-mortar" infrastructure, now a new generation of cheaper and leaner fund companies are seizing market share from the initial fund group leaders. As funds get larger, their costs continue to shrink.

The funds also gain these economies in many other respects, especially when going head-to-head against brokerage firms. Mailing costs, phone reps, research—they're all cheaper for a giant fund complex. As in the software and computer industries, the big are getting bigger—not only individual funds, but fund groups (or families of funds) as well. Because of the deluxe service that customers want—one-stop, all-in-one mutual fund shopping—a few huge no-load fund groups have taken dominant positions. This has also given rise to "mutual fund marketplaces" where shares of many different companies may be purchased in one place; we'll revisit this later.

By pooling people's money and saving on commission costs, mutual funds have become the investment vehicle of choice for the individual investor. Once you've invested their minimum (usually $500 to $5,000), you may purchase shares of a fund, in any amount, whenever you wish. Therefore, you can buy stocks and bonds periodically without being nickel-and-dimed by commission costs, though many funds do now have minimum additional purchase amounts.

Here's another short word about individual stocks. While I think it's fine for investors to take a flier here and there and to have a little fun once in a while, I urge you to limit your exposure to stocks to a small fraction of your long-term investment money (at most). However, alongside a well-diversified portfolio of mutual funds, a downright speculative stock could actually reduce risk (by moving independently to the rest of your holdings—zigging when the portfolio zags). Even so, unless you're already familiar with them and their risks, I suggest you stay away from *individual* stocks.

Diversity, Diversity, Diversity

There is one overriding reason why mutual funds have taken over as the investment vehicle of choice—the diversity they provide makes them extremely safe. Funds aren't totally bulletproof; you can still lose all your money should disaster strike. But they're much safer than any individual stock. Should a disaster big enough to wipe out a broadly diversified mutual fund's entire value occur, your mutual fund will be the last thing you will be worrying about—it would take WWIII or a similar apocalypse.

Their safety comes from numbers. By owning hundreds of securities and by investing in many different industries and geographic locations, the mutual fund dramatically lessens the chance that a single or a small number of bad investments can seriously threaten your portfolio performance. It cannot, of course, protect against a major market decline, but it can shelter you against even an entire industry's fortunes suddenly turning.

In addition to diversity, other major benefits of mutual funds include professional management, liquidity, simplicity, and lower costs.

Professional Management

While in Chapter 6 I will attempt to make an argument for what is known as "indexing," or buying and holding broad baskets of stocks, I still agree that the management of a fund is of utmost importance. Not only is the portfolio manager, the one who's choosing the stocks, bonds, or other investments, important, but the operations, trading, and research team all contribute to the success of any investments. Even with index funds, management plays a crucial role in executing trades and developing the computer models that select the investments. Funds allow investors the muscle to hire professionals.

By pooling resources, investors manage to take advantage of these economies, which allow the fund to get rock-bottom commissions and special treatment when buying and selling shares in the marketplace. This is treatment that none but the largest of individual investors could hope to receive on his or her own.

Liquidity

Most mutual funds may be sold at any time. This beautiful feature of funds is one of the main reasons for their popularity. Though you still get only the day's closing price (if you call before 4 p.m. EST, or whenever the cutoff is), you can call and place the trade anytime. Of course, trading on the Internet could pressure the funds into changing this policy down the road, as computers make possible the calculation of real-time NAVs.

Remember, the fund is priced only once a day, but the underlying assets—the stocks, bonds, cash, and so on—are priced continuously while the market's open. If the market crashes in one day, it's already too late. You'll sell a mutual fund at the closing price for that day. Because of this, you cannot trade the mutual fund markets intra-day, but you shouldn't be timing the market anyway.

Simplicity

As a result of the dawn of toll-free 800 numbers, the buying, selling, and transferring of shares is easier than ever, and with the Internet it'll only get better. An aggressive growth, a growth and income, a real estate, and a money market fund may all be on a one-page statement. Mutual fund companies are known for having some of the best customer service people and techniques of any industry.

Lower Costs

You have professional traders and managers running the fund and customer representatives on 1-800 lines ready to transfer or redeem your shares, 24 hours a day. This pooling of assets and division of labor reduce costs dramatically. No-load mutual funds average somewhere in the neighborhood of 1 percent annually in expenses (depending on the type of funds, company, and more). And some companies average 0.5 percent or less. This is compared to the old-fashioned load funds, some of which charged as much as a 7 percent sales charge, plus up to 2 percent or more in annual expenses.

Money market and bond funds, in particular, are influenced tremendously by expenses. With these funds, the lower costs are passed on directly in the form of higher yields. Even if I don't convince you that expenses are the most important factor in determining returns for stock funds, you shouldn't have much trouble believing that cost is the most important factor with bond and money funds.

Types of Funds

There are now more than 6,000 mutual funds in existence—that's more funds than individual stocks—and hundreds of *types* of funds. Most may be grouped into three broad categories: money market funds, bond funds, and stock funds. There are also various combinations of these as well as specialized funds, such as gold or technology funds. The fund itself is made up of underlying investments—stocks, bonds, whatever, and passes its gains, losses, and/or dividends along directly to the shareholders. With one mutual fund share, you obtain fractional ownership in hundreds of investments.

Before considering the type of fund, you must decide what the fund is for. Short-term goals, such as a down payment for a house in a year, should be placed in money market mutual funds. Figure 5-2 shows the percentages of assets (in total) that investors hold in each type of fund.

As you can see, investors' assets are split fairly evenly among these three classes. Although stocks have the largest portion, this has been the case only over the last year and a half since the market has returned almost 50 percent during that time.

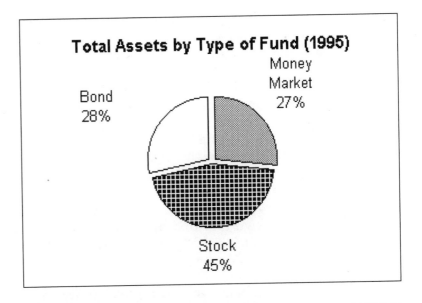

Figure 5-2. Where investors hold their assets.

(Source: (*Investment Company Institute*, 1996 Mutual Fund Fact Book, Washington, DC.).

Money Market Funds

Once we begin our online trading adventures, the first step will be to open up a money market account. For those of you still wondering, a money market mutual fund consists of extremely short-term debt instruments, like U.S. Treasury bills or large-denomination certificates of deposits (CDs); it is the mutual fund equivalent of cash. Money funds are the safest of investments. They consistently maintain a $1 per share NAV (net asset value) or price, credit interest payments daily (but pay this out or reinvest it in additional shares monthly), and can be redeemed at $1.00 a share—always.

Money funds' main attraction lies in their safety and liquidity. Most accounts have check-writing privileges, so investors may access their funds any time. And, a stable $1.00 a share NAV means that there won't be any loss of your original investment. Though not guaranteed by the government, this $1.00 NAV has become gospel in the industry. It is highly unlikely that any reputable money fund will ever "break the buck." Of course, you can always stick with the largest companies and/or 100 percent U.S. Treasury funds, which invest in only the highest-rated short-term investments, for an added degree of protection.

Money funds' average maturity (or the length of time when the investments will have come due, or paid back their principal) must be 90 days or less. They can't invest in anything with more than a 13-month maturity. It is true, however, that they're not FDIC insured. But compared to stocks and bonds, they're as safe as Fort Knox.

The best use of a money market fund (not to be confused with a bank money market deposit account, MMDA, which *is* insured) is as a parking place for cash while it's awaiting investment opportunities. You'll earn more than the interest rates on CDs, and these funds are exceptionally safe. Even longer-term investors should consider money funds if they require absolute safety.

Yes, there have been some cases of money market funds threatening to lose money ("break the buck" or drop below $1.00 a share in net asset value), but those were tiny funds; these cases also occurred before new, more restrictive regulations were put in place. Stick with the big funds anyway, though, so you're ready to invest in stock or bond funds gradually.

A few good places to start when looking for a money fund are the largest ones: Vanguard Prime Portfolio Money Market Portfolio, Fidelity Cash Reserves, Schwab Money Market Fund, Strong MMF, or Dreyfus MMF. While you might find a money fund that is yielding a bit more than these, it's doubtful that the additional pay-out would be enough to compensate for the added risk a smaller fund family brings.

Money funds have the lowest expense ratios of all mutual funds. Even though expenses matter because they can eat up a significant amount of the interest earned, convenience and proximity to stock and bond funds should be significant considerations. Note: Fidelity, Vanguard, and Schwab are all low cost and have extensive services, such as check writing, wire transfers, and more, so I'll concentrate on these three companies for examples and recommendations.

Bond Funds

Also known as fixed-income funds because of their predictable dividend payments, bond funds are fairly conservative on the risk spectrum. Of course, just how conservative depends on what types of bond funds you're talking about. They range from short-term bond funds, which are only slightly riskier than money market funds, to the long-term bond funds, whose principal can fluctuate dramatically. Investors looking for predictable, though still variable, dividend payments and income should consider bond funds. A rule of thumb for which type of fund is right: The sooner you'll need the money, the shorter the term (maturity or duration) of your fund should be.

Some financial advisors and brokers claim that individual bonds are better than bond funds due to the predictable dividend payment stream of the single bond. But I think, for most purposes, the fund is simpler. Fund expenses are far lower than commissions on individual bonds for most. And the bond fund's check-writing privileges make them downright liquid. Especially for investors looking for income, bond funds make plenty of sense.

Short-term bond funds usually pay less income than, but don't fluctuate nearly as much in price as longer-term bonds. Investors should decide between money market funds and short-term bond funds, or a combination of both, for money held for anywhere from one day to five years. What is called average maturity (AM) determines how long-term your bond fund is; the sooner you need the money, the shorter your AM should be.

Another option for investors looking for a little growth with their income is the *hybrid bond and stock fund*, which invests mainly in bonds but also invests a minority of its assets in dividend-paying stocks. These are sometimes known as income funds, though some "income" funds invest totally in stocks.

Vanguard's Wellesley Income is an example of the former type of fund—it's made up of 60 percent investment-grade (high-quality) corporate bonds and 40 percent high-dividend stocks. It is the perfect conservative income vehicle for those entering retirement. There are many more funds that are more stocks than bonds; these are touched on below.

Finally, high-yield, or "junk," bond funds, like Fidelity Capital & Income Fund, pay higher dividends but take more risk. Like many more aggressive investments, though, if they're included as a small piece of a diversified portfolio they'll add a nice boost to your income stream. Retirees should be careful with these, though, and keep their allocation small. The additional income may be nice, but preservation of principal should be their prime directive.

Other variations on bond funds include convertible funds, which own bonds that can be converted into stocks (making the fund a blend of both), and preferred funds, which own higher-dividend-paying (more bond-like) stocks.

Stock Funds

Stock funds range from the most conservative, such as income or total stock market index funds, to the most aggressive, like small company or technology-laden growth funds. While every long-term investor should own some stock funds, I must warn you that you invest in stocks for only short periods at your own risk.

Here is a partial listing of types of stock funds:

- Aggressive Growth: These funds either are very actively managed or buy thinly traded and volatile small company stocks (or both).

- Small Company: These funds can range from the most speculative to not-so-speculative (like very broad, small company index funds). Sometimes the terms "aggressive growth" and "small company" are used interchangeably when describing funds, but there may be differences (i.e., pay attention to the fund's holdings).

- Growth: These funds own a broadly diversified basket of stocks. A growth fund can range from very aggressive to very conservative, depending on what sector of the market most of its holdings are from; this is the most common type of stock fund.

- Growth & Income: These funds own mostly conservative "blue-chip" stocks that pay large dividends and may include some bonds.

- Equity-Income: This type owns bonds, along with high-dividend stocks.

- International: These funds are often among the most speculative funds, especially if an emerging market or regional international fund.

- Other: These funds are concentrated "sector" funds of many types, some of which are as dangerous as individual stocks. We'll revisit some of these along with the fund group sites.

Usually, a broadly diversified growth fund, like Fidelity Growth Company or Twentieth Century Ultra, is the best vehicle for long-term investors. While I prefer index funds, and in particular Vanguard's Total Stock Market Index, any fund with hundreds of different stocks should do. They all should perform similarly over time. Young investors with 401(k) plans or IRAs should just choose a good one, and wait 20 years or more.

Over 90 percent of a fund investor's returns can be traced to its asset class (whether it's a stock, bond, or money fund) as opposed to the specific investments, according to the experts. Individual picks account for only 10 percent, believe it or not. What this means is that the overall direction of the market carries a far heavier weight than the talent of any individual manager. This is one reason why I like index funds—they make sure you're gaining exposure to that asset class.

Vanguard Total Stock Market Index is the ultimate stock index fund. It parallels the Wilshire 5000 Index—the broadest of stock market measures, representing 97 percent of the publicly traded stock in the country. This fund is for investors who admit that they're helpless against the market's fickle swings between sectors and industries. This fund also makes sure that you won't miss another rally. It's invested everywhere, at least in the United States. We'll return to growth and stock funds in coming chapters.

Funds of Funds

A fund of funds is just what it sounds like; it's a meta-fund. It is made up of several other individual funds, from all stock funds, to stock and bond funds, and so on. This is one of the fastest-growing segments of the mutual fund industry because it attempts to give investors an easy, and often safe, choice. While many financial advisors and writers have derided this category as oversimplified and have criticized the flagship of this sector, Fidelity Asset Manager, I think "funds-of-funds" are fabulous. I think either a fund of funds or a straight growth fund should be your first mutual fund investment. You may even end up needing only one fund.

These funds should be an easy answer when you ask yourself: "What fund should I buy?" or "Where should I invest?" My favorite mutual fund recommendation over the years has been Vanguard STAR Fund. I love this fund because it offers an insane amount of instant diversification. It is the *premier fund of funds.* It's only holdings are nine other Vanguard funds. These include: several growth funds, bond funds, *and* a money market fund, making it one of the best "balanced" funds out there. (A balanced fund keeps constant percentages, i.e., 60 percent stock, 40 percent bond, always.) There are, however, other respectable entrants in the balanced, fund of funds area.

Vanguard LIFEStrategy Funds (Conservative, Growth, and Moderate varieties) and Vanguard Balanced Index are other choices, as are T. Rowe Price Spectrum Growth and Fidelity Puritan. One or two of these, or their equivalents at other fund families, should be the "core" for any large-sum portfolios (perhaps with a large portion bought up front, and the remainder invested over a couple of years). A fund that's extremely well diversified (owning stocks and bonds) should be at the core of every investor's long-term portfolio.

The advantages of balanced funds or *"super-indexed" portfolios* are as follows:

- Fixed fund percentages—They force you to buy into declining sectors. The key to good returns is keeping fixed amounts in several different funds.

- Asset allocation—Though the balanced fund is in fixed percentages, it "rebalances" itself periodically to move back to its target percentages following appreciation or declines in its securities.

Other Investment Vehicles

New hybrids and new fund types are, of course, being created all the time. One recent addition to the "other" category of fund types, like gold, energy, or sector funds, is the REIT fund. Real estate investment trusts invest in equities that gain payments from commercial real estate rent. A REIT fund may help add some diversity to your portfolio, but it should be limited to a fraction of your overall holdings, such as 10 percent for income.

Of course, besides mutual funds made up of REITs or specialized industry stocks, there are thousands of different investments altogether, such as options, futures, and more. Don't invest in them. Or if you must, know the risks, and limit your exposure to a fraction of your long-term investment assets.

The Big No-Load Fund Groups, Discount Brokers, and Services

There remain thousands of choices as far as mutual funds go, but you probably are invested in or considering only a handful. Over the past decade, Fidelity Investments has become the largest mutual fund company in the world; it could eventually become the largest financial services company. It has done so primarily on performance, but it couldn't have been so successful without excellent service and an extensive lineup of funds and investment products. As the reigning

Empire, therefore, Fidelity remains choice number one for millions of investors.

The other big no-load choices are quickly being reduced to two—Schwab or Vanguard. Sure, there are other fund groups with excellent products, among them T. Rowe Price, Twentieth Century/Benham, Dreyfus/Mellon, Scudder, Oakmark, Montgomery, Strong, and others. These companies do good jobs. But the importance of being able to get everything at one place grows. More and more investors want simplicity—a single statement, plus the availability of any kind of fund that you might possibly need. Because performance is so dependent on the market, being able to be in a *specific* fund is less important than it once was.

The giants of the fund industry, Fidelity and Vanguard, and the mutual fund "supermarkets," like Schwab, and discount broker Jack White, get bigger. They are definitely the only place you need to go for your investments, and with their dominance of the 401(k) plan market you may well already be investing with them. You'll see shortly that these companies were on the Web early. Their presence is unavoidable in the new medium.

Goldman Sachs predicted a while back that many of today's fund companies would be gone—merged or taken over—by the year 2000. Because they expect the costs of obtaining and retaining investment assets to continue climbing substantially, they feel that only the giants will survive. With the onslaught of online investing, size will matter even more as people look for a dependable name backing their mutual electronic billions.

Already, Schwab is beginning to sell no-load, variable (fund-like) life insurance. Can full-service checking accounts be far behind? As barriers of regulation fall in various financial industries, these large mutual fund companies look very well positioned to become the one-stop financial supermarket site of the future. Certainly, the full-service brokers, insurance agents, and others aren't going anywhere just yet, but competition among financial behemoths is certain to accelerate.

It Matters:
Loads, Fees, and Costs

Of course, the reason that so many mutual funds have come into existence in the past few years is that the business is so profitable. Even the no-load funds have to make their money somewhere, so it's important for you to be aware of where they do it. There are several types of fees and several layers of fees.

Loads/Sales Charges

In case you haven't noticed yet, I am no fan of loads. My investing examples and suggestions recommend only no-load funds because I feel that the last thing you should be paying for is to let someone else hold your money. For some investors, though, paying a load might not be so bad. If you have a good advisor who's earning the fee, stay on target. It's far more important to invest in the first place than it is to decide who to invest with. Keep in mind that you can probably find a similar-enough fund without the load, no matter what kind of fund you're talking about.

The total load paid may be found by taking the difference between NAV (net asset value), or the sell price of the fund, and the buy price of the fund—the total cost to you per share. Subtract the sale price (NAV) from the buy price (offer price) to get the sales charge, then divide the sales charge by the buy price to get the percentage load paid (i.e., Offer price – NAV / Offering price = Sales Load %).

It often pays to have professional advice, but some of these loads of 4 percent or more can really put you in the red. Watch out for banks and brokers—not to mention insurance people; if they're getting a big commission, you may be paying too much. For some well-managed growth funds the load may be well worth it, but over time big charges are guaranteed to eat heavily into your returns.

12b-1 Fees

Another variation of the sales charge is the 12b-1 fee, which is added annually to expenses. It pays for distribution costs, and it goes either directly to the company or to the broker (if sold by one). I advise avoiding any funds with 12b-1 fees. Almost always, you can find a similar-enough alternate without the fee. Note that changes in 12b-1 fees must be approved by fund shareholders.

Annual Management Fees

These are the annual charges, as a percentage of your assets, that go to pay administration costs. You can't avoid them, but you shouldn't be paying more than 1 percent or 1.5 percent annually. And even that's a little high for my taste. You can find fund groups whose fees average well under 1 percent annually. Information about fund expenses may be found in the prospectus, and it is available on most of these companies' Web sites already. Finally, the last word on fees: if you're making a lot of money and are happy, relax—you're fine.

Performance Measurement

No matter what the investment—an emerging market stock fund, a money market fund, whatever—the number one test as to whether it's a good fund is always performance, or total return. How much money did it make? The first thing most people ask when considering a fund is: "How's its performance?" People are attracted to performance more than anything, but I urge you to consider other factors first, like the expense ratio of the fund and whether it sticks with its stated strategy.

At the very least, determine *why* the performance was what it was. Could your blue-chip growth stock fund be number one because it's chosen the right sector of the economy to invest in, or has it been dabbling in some esoteric investments, like Japanese yen futures? *No fund's performance should stray too far from that of its peers.* Of course, you need to know how to measure performance first.

Total return is the current or end price minus the initial or buy price, plus any dividends or capital gains reinvested in additional shares. It is most often seen in an annualized format, unless the time period examined is less than a year, in which case it should not be annualized. Funds usually list their one-year, three-year, five-year, and other *annualized* returns. Performance should be looked at on both an absolute and a relative basis—whether your fund beat its peers should be as important as whether it made money.

Just be careful about outrageous claims. Keep in mind that many times the numbers aren't what they seem. Listen carefully for what time period the performance number covers, how it was calculated, and whether it is annualized. Finally, whenever you hear investment "systems" that make outrageous claims about 1,000 percent-plus returns, listen as to whether any of their "proof" was with theoretical or real dollars. And in either case, be skeptical.

6

Investing Strategies

Now that you're familiar with investing and mutual funds, it's time to put some of this knowledge to use. Let's move on to investing strategies—how to decide *when to buy, which funds to buy,* and *how much to buy of each fund.* Every investment is different, but the following techniques, guidelines, and principles should give you an excellent starting point for building or remodeling a winning portfolio of mutual funds. After this chapter, you're on your own as far as advice goes.

Almost every investor seeks spectacular returns. But most also expect to perform well consistently. Unfortunately, there is no secret to riches. No system or strategy is foolproof although you wouldn't know it from some marketing pitches. Investors seeking easy money have been having as difficult a time as Lord Bowen's metaphysician: "A blind man in a dark room—looking for a black hat—which isn't there."

Well, I'm going to tell you that you're looking for the wrong hat, that you're in the wrong room, and that the light switch is on the wall. There's no secret way to easy money, but there are tried-and-true principles to help guide you to consistent and decent returns. These are examined later in this chapter.

First, I review some of the predominant schools of thought in mutual fund investing today, then concentrate on a few simple strategies. I also show you why it is impossible to consistently "beat" the market, or at the very least, why it is far wiser for you to take the safer path of *matching the market*. It may not be as exciting, but I think that you'll be better off financially. And you'll probably sleep better, too.

Even as the no-load mutual fund industry expanded dramatically over the past 30 years, the regulations surrounding the funds made it difficult to obtain specific advice from the fund families themselves. If you didn't have a broker's or advisor's guidance, you had to sort through newspapers, newsletters, magazines, and specialized data sources to make your own decisions. Or, you've had to rely on the kindness of strangers. Some of these sources could have interests in mind other than your own.

Thankfully, that is changing. Financial planners and fee-for-service programs are proliferating, and the big no-load companies are moving further into the advice arena. In addition to their all-in-one balanced and broadly diversified growth-stock funds, Vanguard, Fidelity, and Schwab are establishing various "cookie-cutter" plans; these involve questionnaires that automatically suggest a mix of funds. Web-based "fund allocators" are already in place at most of the larger fund groups' sites. We'll return to this topic in Chapter 10.

These recommendations make excellent starting points and, with a little help along the way, should be enough for most beginners. Once these suggestions are coupled with the information available on various World Wide Web sites, there is no reason why you shouldn't succeed as your own investment advisor.

Any recommendations you get, you'll want to cross-reference with an independent source. While a visit to the financial planner may well be in order for more complicated investment needs, I'll give you a quick and simple outline for building a portfolio of funds right here. Just keep in mind that any investment decision is always your own (i.e., I hold no responsibility for any losses!). Novice investors should take it slow.

The Long-Term Investment "Core"

Any long-term investment strategy should comprise primarily stock, bond, and money market mutual funds—both in retirement plans (401(k), company pension, or other) and in taxable accounts. But it should also take into account real estate (primarily a house), emergency cash, and more. Before making any investment, you must carefully consider the makeup of your current assets, or "asset allocation"— be they stocks, bonds, or cash—and whether you're over- or underweighted in any particular area. Any financial planning should start with a thorough inventory of where you are now.

The information and recommendations contained herein are aimed at what I call nonessential investments. In other words, all of the money that is to be put toward these mutual funds or other investments should be money you won't need to survive on because, as I've said, the key to capital growth is the compounding of interest over time. You want any investment money to be invested for a very long time, if not forever.

For long-term or retirement money, most investment texts suggest a portfolio composed of somewhere in the neighborhood of 60 percent stock investments, 25 percent bond investments, 10 percent international (stocks), and 5 percent cash—always. These are general guidelines for investment planning, but feel free to strive for a decent return at a moderate risk level. I suggest starting conservatively, then seeking out your own level of comfort. Most investment advisors suggest long-term blends ranging from around 40 percent stocks to as much as 90 percent, but the average is around 60 to 70 percent stocks. In the long run, the more stock you have, the better. The important thing, though, is just to get started.

Your investment "core" should be a diversified growth fund and a bond fund (or a balanced fund that covers both of these). A common mistake is to have too many funds; more than 10 is definitely too many. The "core" funds should be extremely diversified—the fund should own more than 200 different stocks—and conservative. Especially suited for a large portion of this stock segment are index funds, which mirror a widely watched financial index, or "blue-chip," high-quality growth funds.

As mentioned, Vanguard Total Stock Market Index Fund is the ultimate choice for the stock core. It mirrors the Wilshire

5000 Index, the broadest of market barometers, representing approximately 97 percent of all U.S. stocks. The Vanguard Index 500 Fund is another example. It comprises all of the stocks making up the Standard & Poor's 500 Index, which is second only to the Dow Jones Industrial Average in popularity as far as indexes go. It represents shares in approximately 70 percent of *all* the publicly owned companies in the United States. Other excellent index fund choices include Fidelity Market Index Fund and the Schwab 1000 Index Fund. These funds should all track the entire "stock market" quite closely.

If you don't like indexes, any big, well-known growth fund will do just fine. Examples of these include Fidelity Contrafund, Vanguard U.S. Growth, and Montgomery Growth. Unless you choose an exceptionally aggressive or conservative growth stock fund, its returns shouldn't vary much from the broader market's.

While index investors should be fine with just one stock fund, those using actively-managed funds should probably diversify among styles (small stock versus large stock or value versus growth) by investing in more than one fund. This way, you won't miss out on an unexpected shift in market sentiment.

Depending on where you are in your investment "life-cycle," the next fund for your "core" should be anything from a growth and income fund to an aggressive growth stock fund. This fund's main purpose is to diversify your stock holdings even further. For example, a 30-year-old investor might add Vanguard Small Cap Index while a 60-year-old might add Fidelity Growth and Income. This second fund, which isn't really necessary if the first fund is broad enough, adds another degree of safety to the portfolio.

To complete the "core," you'll need a diversified bond fund as well. Vanguard's Fixed-Income Long-Term Investment

Grade Bond Fund or Wellesley Income Fund (see below) are excellent examples of this. This bond portion of your portfolio is there to provide stability and security to your assets, and to generate steady income. While those investors with decades until retirement won't need this fund, most will. The amount allocated here should be increased along with an investor's age.

These funds are mere examples, so feel free to substitute the same class or type of fund from your own fund family. (Also, the balanced funds I spoke of in Chapter 5, Vanguard STAR, Fidelity Puritan, and Vanguard Balanced Index, among others, make perfect "instant cores" for the smaller investor.) Once you've established these objectives, you can then branch out into international funds, gold funds, and individual stocks, secure in the knowledge that you're well shielded from the unpredictability of the market.

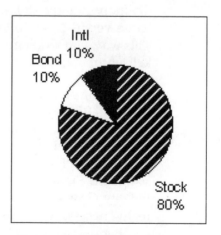

Figure 6-1a. 20-year old.

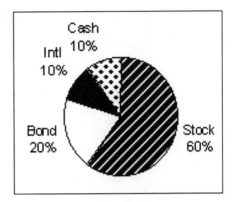

Figure 6-1b. 45-year old.

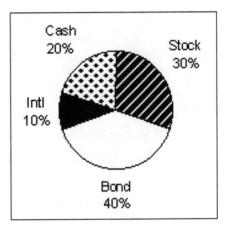

Figure 6-1c. 70-year old.

Following are my sample funds to fulfill the aforementioned suggested asset allocations, but, again, feel free to substitute your own favorites. Also feel free to adjust the percentages, depending on your comfort level.

Sample Recommended Fund Portfolios

		Vanguard Fund	Fidelity Fund	Schwab Fund
Figure 6-1a	10%	International Index	Overseas	International Index
	10%	Total Bond Market Index	Intermediate Bond	Long-Term Govt. Bond
	80%	Total Stock Market Index	Market Index	1000 Index
Figure 6-1b	10%	Prime Port. Money Market	Cash Reserves	Money Market
	10%	International Index	Overseas	International Index
	20%	Total Bond Market Index	Intermediate Bond	Long-Term Govt. Bond
	60%	Total Stock Market Index	Market Index	1000 Index
Figure 6-1c	20%	Prime Port. Money Market	Cash Reserves	Money Market
	10%	International Index	Overseas	International Index
	40%	Total Bond Market Index	Intermediate Bond	Long-Term Govt. Bond
	30%	Total Stock Market Index	Market Index	1000 Index

Remember, any allocation should depend on your primary reasons or goals for investing—college tuition in 10 years, retirement in 15 years, and so on—and adjusted accordingly. The closer the due date, the safer and shorter should be your investments. I mentioned the rule for estimating the amount you should have invested in stock funds: 100 minus your age. This percentage will give you another general guideline to judge whether your own percentage is heavy or light on stock funds or on bond funds. But feel free to find your own comfort level.

Investment Types: Fundamental, Technical, Other

Already, you've been exposed to my prejudices regarding investing, so I want to review some of the other schools of thought. While there are two broad types, there are countless other minor variations. Most investors use a complicated blend of many different philosophies when choosing investments. You'll encounter debates about investment philosophy on newsgroups, chat rooms, and bulletin boards, but you'll eventually get a feel for what "type" of investor you are.

- Fundamental analysis—The study of corporate earnings and balance sheets, as well as the economy and interest rates. This is the dominant method by which most stocks and funds are analyzed.

- Technical analysis—The study of price and volume movements and charts. You'll see an awful lot of technical followers among discussion groups. Believe it or not, some devotees of technical analysis would buy a stock not even knowing the name of a company or what industry it's in!

Each belief has advantages, and each can provide insight into the behavior of a security or a market reaction to certain news items. You'll encounter these terms repeatedly at investment areas of the Internet.

Other types of investment-philosophy "schools of thought" are as follows:

- Contrarian investors would be interested, perhaps, in a stock whose price has recently broken a moving average (recent average price) on the *downside*. They like downtrodden areas and turnarounds; similar to "value investors."

- Value investors look for bargains (whereas contrarians would like expensive stocks if no one else did!). Common measures of value include: cheap price-to-book value ratios, low price-to-earnings (P/E) ratios, high dividends, and many more.

- Growth investors like things that go up or have steady earnings and/or dividend growth. They especially like *increasing* earnings at companies and the potential for "home runs" (stocks that quadruple or go up by huge amounts).

Dollar-Cost Averaging

When thinking about investing, second only to "Which fund should I buy?" is often the question, "How should I buy it?" Should I dive right into the market or wait to buy? By far, the safest method is to dollar-cost average, or to invest gradually. You automatically do this with 401(k)s or monthly savings plans, adding so much each paycheck. This averages out the price you pay for your shares, lowering your costs overall (at least, once you've fulfilled the minimum requirements). In buying shares of mutual funds (or stocks) over time, more shares are bought at a lower price.

Here's an example: Suppose you invest $100 in a hypothetical "The Internet Fund" at $15 a share, and you do the same the next two months at $5 and $10 a share, respectively. Over three months you've purchased:

Month #1	6 ⅔ shares for $100 (at $15/share)
Month #2	20 shares for $100 (at $5/share)
Month #3	10 shares for $100 (at $10/share)
Total:	36 ⅔ shares; worth $366.66 at current price of $10 a share

If you had bought all your shares at $10, the average price, you'd have only 30 shares ($300 worth) of the fund. In other words, in this way you buy more shares when the price is lower.

Another reason dollar-cost averaging is great is that it gives you an automatic investment cash source. It may be diverted should you need the money; you can stop contributing and divert this cash to your needs, as opposed to selling a portion of your investments. Of course, a heavy cash reserve is always desirable. Your investment purchases don't have to be made right away, and you'll possess a great advantage over other investors by having cash ready to invest on market weakness. This money should be poised to take advantage of a market crash or other good investment opportunity.

Weighted Dollar-Cost Averaging

If you're just starting out investing in mutual funds and have a substantial lump sum to begin with, I also recommend the strategy of *weighted dollar-cost averaging*. This strategy couples dollar-cost averaging, or investing a fixed-dollar amount each month, with a lump sum up front. By investing a large percentage, say a quarter (25 percent), up front, *you instantly put some money to work in your diversified portfolio, but you also protect the bulk of your savings from buying in at a market high.* You can vary the amount invested initially and the amount invested each month according to your own taste.

Start with the "core" funds, then add the other funds for diversification as additional cash becomes available. Once you've established your initial portfolio of funds, place the remaining three-quarters (75 percent) into a money fund (such as Vanguard Prime Portfolio—Money Market Fund) and establish a monthly transfer into the stock and bond funds. This safe and easy tactic gives you the best of both worlds—market exposure *and* safety.

Types of Dollar-Cost Averaging

Two different ways for you to average your investments are buying a fixed number of shares per month (10 shares or so, depending on share price) or investing a fixed-dollar amount ($100 or so) per month. These methods of investing in mutual funds have proven to be safe, reliable ways of growing a successful portfolio.

Fixed-Dollar Amounts

Investing a fixed-dollar amount each month into one or more mutual funds is known as dollar-cost averaging. This forces the discipline needed to buy in good times and in bad, especially the bad. Investing $100, $500, or whatever every month into several well-diversified mutual funds is the easy way to wealth.

Fixed-Share Amounts

An alternative strategy is to buy a fixed number of shares each month. Here you would buy, say, 10 shares of a $10 fund each month, but you'd continue buying 10 shares even if the price went to $8 a share (or to $12). Whatever the current price is, you'll be varying your dollar amounts each month—investing more in shares going up and less in shares going down.

Both of these strategies shield you from overpaying, but investing equal dollar amounts is the more effective strategy in almost every type of market.

Indexing: Surviving the Random Walk

One of the major themes of this investing section is that *indexing*, or linking your investments to the entire market, is one of the easiest, safest, and yet most effective investment strategies available. It basically guarantees fund performance that matches an index; this strategy has consistently beaten 70 percent or so of all growth funds. After expenses and commissions are accounted for, most other funds can't beat index funds. Why?

- Low Costs: Most stock funds that are actively managed charge annual fees of 1 percent or more, with some charging over 2 percent per year due to their higher commission and research costs. Non-index funds often trade their portfolios heavily, which also causes excess tax consequences—capital gains that are taken must be distributed.

- Low Risk: Of course, there's nowhere to hide in a major market downturn or crash, but indexing can help you avoid being in the wrong sector of the market. You won't be among the top-performing funds if you index, but you won't be at the bottom either. And you won't be caught investing in the "hottest" sector of the market, only to see your fund drop 20 percent as another type of fund assumes leadership.

- Always Invested: This is my personal favorite. Nothing makes me madder than a fund that misses out on a big market rally. Index funds don't have to worry about poor market timing and don't have to worry about missing the turnaround sectors.

- Guaranteed Returns: Because the general trend of the stock market remains upward, you want to make sure that your investments are constantly gaining ground. By indexing all, or at least a "core" of your portfolio, you'll make sure that the market doesn't leave you behind.

Of course, even if you're convinced that indexing is indeed a valid strategy, there remains the question of *which* index or indexes to follow. While by far the most famous is the Standard & Poor's 500 Stock Index (the 500 largest companies in the United States), there are both broader and more concentrated index funds, as well as overseas, real estate investment trust (REIT), bond, and other index funds. As I mentioned, a broader U.S. stock market index, such as Vanguard Total Stock Market Index, is probably the best choice.

Keep in mind that even though I'm blatantly partisan in my fund selection, any lower-cost, broadly diversified fund is fine. Unless its investment strategy is dramatically different from that of most other funds, its performance will approximate the index. The more stocks or bonds it owns, by definition, the closer its performance will be to an index. So, rest easy. Just being invested in any fund is the most important factor in investing.

Finally, indexing is in its incipient stages. Only a small fraction of investors have yet to give up their quixotic quest for superior returns. As Vanguard's John Bogle said recently on the subject, "We know that indexed assets presently represent about 25 percent of the assets of corporate pension plans and about 6 percent of the assets of 401(k) plans. So, there is enormous room for growth in index funds. An increase to even a 15 percent penetration would raise assets of equity index mutual funds from $70 billion today to $250 billion, assuming no change in industry equity assets. We shall see." Given the performance of the Vanguard Index 500 against other growth stock funds over the past two years and Fidelity Magellan's poor showing, I expect Vanguard's Index 500 to overtake Magellan as the largest stock fund within the next five years.

As a side note: Burton G. Malkiel, author *A Random Walk Down Wall Street*, is the father of indexing. His book discusses the entire field of investments in detail, as well as the "random walk" theory of stock prices. This theory proposes that stock prices will move in a random direction and that throwing darts at the stock listings would give you the same chances as investment professionals. This occurs because all of the information available about a stock should already be reflected in the stock price and is the theoretical foundation behind indexing. For those interested, Malkiel's book is one of the best texts available for any investors, from novice to professional.

A Fool and His Money ...

Here I wanted to briefly comment on *The Motley Fool Investment Guide* by David and Tom Gardner. First off, it's a good book with plenty of sound investment advice. Their discussion and refinement of the "Dogs of the Dow" strategy, whereby investors buy the highest-yielding stocks among the Dow Jones Industrial Average (the most beaten-up of companies), is excellent and very sound investment advice. But their advocacy of highly volatile, small, technology companies for the individual investor is dangerous, and their urging that anyone can beat the indexes is a pipe dream.

There may indeed somewhere be a way to make more money than the market with less risk, but it's never been done consistently. Consider the way famous investors Peter Lynch and Warren Buffet are lionized for beating the S&P 500 by a couple percentage points—can you name even one or two others who've done this? Anyone beating the market begins to attract copycats and assets, which will eventually return them to the mean. (*The Motley Fool*'s Website is covered briefly in Chapter 13.)

Just a reminder, while I firmly believe in my recommendations, you're the one who has to live with your investment choices. Many observers consider my approach too conservative or simplistic; I consider those criticisms compliments. This is just one view of the investment world; there are thousands of others. I'm sure you'll find a few good fund companies and information providers that you'll be comfortable with in the following chapters.

Mutual Fund Investing on the Internet's "10 Rules of Investing"

1. Never chase performance.

2. Dollar-cost average (invest every month).

3. Don't try to time the market.

4. Buy and hold … forever.

5. Stick with indexes.

6. Diversify among securities *and* asset classes.

7. Don't pay loads, 12b-1 fees, or excessive fees.

8. Balanced funds are okay.

9. The simpler, the better.

10. Maximize tax-deferred options.

Cyberglossary

Because there exist so many excellent glossaries on mutual funds and financial terms on the World Wide Web, I decided just to point you toward several online glossaries that I feel are both comprehensive and understandable.

Fund Co. /Organization	Address
AAII	http://www.aaii.org/glossary.html
Altamira	http://www.altamira.com/altamira/library/gloss2.html
CNBC	http://www.cnbc.com/tickerguide/termin.html
Federal Reserve	http://woodrow.mpls.frb.fed.us/banking/mutual/glossary.html
Galaxy (Fleet)	http://www.fleet.com/persbank/invstmnt/mutfun/mutglo.html
Mutual Fund Education Alliance	http://www.mfea.com/glssindx.html
Prudential	http://www.prusec.com/glos_txt.html
Schwab	http://www.schwab.com/SchwabNOW/SNLibrary/SNLib014/SN014.html
SteinRoe	http://networth.galt.com/www/home/mutual/steinroe/glossary.html
Twentieth Century	http://www.twentieth-century.com/section5/5-1/index.html

Part III

Onto the Net

The next three chapters are a warm-up before we get into evaluating mutual fund company and related Web sites. First, Chapter 7 discusses getting connected and the pros and cons of Internet service providers versus the online services (for those who are really new to the Internet). We'll also briefly examine the proprietary investment areas of the major online services.

Though we're focusing on the World Wide Web, there are extensive mutual fund and investing resources on each of the online services. Any guide to investment resources would not be complete without mention of the investing sections at America Online, CompuServe, and Prodigy. And because this is where many readers started out, I begin here.

Chapter 8 moves on to Data and Searching, giving strategies for finding particular investment topics or companies. This overview is also meant for the more junior surfers among you. It sets a good foundation for the specific site sections that follow. The search engines and starting points mentioned also have many investment resources of their own, so we'll review the major ones. In addition, this chapter discusses "agents" and "off-line" services; developing alternatives to traditional search methods.

Chapter 9 moves into the major news, magazine, and other information sites that specialize in investing. Here, too, I discuss developing areas, such as personalized news sources and premium services. Though not essential for longer-term investors, these sites are among the best and most useful on the Web.

It's a given that there is enough useful information on the Internet. The challenge is finding it quickly and efficiently. Before we move onto the specific fund company and other Web sites, I want to be sure you're familiar with the various search engines and types of information available on the Internet. Then, we'll move into the hardcore investing sites.

7

Online Services

Within the last 15 years, America Online, CompuServe, and Prodigy have grown from zero subscribers to over 10 million. Internet users number in the tens of millions worldwide; the online-service user community represents the majority of these within the United States. The demise of online services has been predicted for years now, but they've managed not only to survive but to prosper. They're still adding new subscribers at healthy rates (though not as fast as direct providers are), and each of them offers an array of excellent investment resources.

However, these online service providers (OSPs, as opposed to ISPs—Internet service providers, like Netcom or GNN) are losing customers almost as fast as they're signing them up. As their users become computer savvy and rack up some rather large usage bills, they've been migrating to the cheaper ISPs. A recent *Wall Street Journal* article sums up the dilemma facing the online services. It quoted Jonathan Cohen, a managing director at Smith Barney: "The Internet is siphoning off prospective online service customers from companies like CompuServe…. The price of direct access to the Internet is continuing to fall, and functionality of the World Wide Web is improving."

Another *Journal* article opined, "Now the services risk getting crushed by the craze they helped create, as the Internet and its snazzy World Wide Web area outgrow even the most buoyant forecasts." It also quoted Forrester Research analyst William Bluestein as saying the online services better develop Internet skills fast, "or they'll get blown out of the water."

While this was, and to a degree still is, the case, the online services have countered forcefully. Though many of the more technically savvy scorn them, the online services—America Online, CompuServe, and Prodigy—have some of the best investment news, information, and advice around.

They definitely provide an easier means of putting yourself into an investment environment where you can wander around, and their news features remain slightly ahead of the Internet. Thus, a good portion of this chapter reviews some of the online services' fund, investment information, and trading offerings. First, though, let's start with the pros and cons of ISPs versus OSPs.

ISPs: The Death of Online Services?

For many, the cheaper and faster "ticket to the I-Way" has been the Internet service providers, like Netcom, GNN (Global Network Navigator, now owned by America Online), or local providers, such as TIAC (The Internet Access Company) in Boston. Now, the giants of telecommunications—AT&T, MCI, and Sprint—are getting into the act as well. These companies have seen the threat posed by ISPs and have countered by giving away hours of free access. Which of the variations will survive is difficult to guess, but for now it appears that the biggies are here to stay.

Just a reminder: for direct Internet access, your service provider has no effect on a site's content; only the browser effects the actual appearance of Web sites. However, some ISPs are adding personalized services, such as custom news and more, which are available only to their own subscribers. While some ISPs do have investment resources of their own, most do not. These are noted below in my brief review of each.

- AT&T—The long distance giant stunned the ISP world when it announced that it would enter the field and give away five hours of access per month. However, AT&T was plagued by delays and problems getting started. Nonetheless, as the largest telecommunications company in the world, expect AT&T to be a major force on the Internet.

  For occasional Web users, you can't beat AT&T's five-hours-free deal, though how long this pricing can last remains to be seen. AT&T had been distributing

Netscape's browser, but it now appears to be shifting to Microsoft's Internet Explorer.

- Netcom—This was one of the early providers on the Net and remains the biggest independent Internet access company. Like some of the other ISPs, Netcom has been building up its own content areas to establish a stronger brand name.

- GNN—Owned by America Online, this access provider may gradually be integrated into AOL. GNN is one of the few ISPs with its own content, including GNN's Personal Finance Center and the Whole Internet Catalog. I review the Personal Finance Center in Chapter 13.

- Others: IDT, PSINet, UUNet, Sprynet, The Well, TIAC (The Internet Access Company), regional providers, etc.—Investment resources will vary. MCI and Sprint also have or are planning access packages.

Tables 7-1 and 7-2 will assist you in comparing the different services on price and access, but you should stick with the vendor with whom you feel most comfortable. (Personally, I'm happy with Netcom, but I need the unlimited access price.)

Table 7-1 Online Service Providers

	# of Users	800#	Pricing	Rating
America Online	6.2 mil.	827-6364	$19.95 (20 hrs) + $2.95/hr or $9.95 (5 hrs) + 2.95/hr	@@

Gets expensive for heavy users.

Table 7-1 Continued

	# of Users	800#	Pricing	Rating
CompuServe	3.4 mil.	336-6823	$9.95 (5 hrs) + $2.95/hr	@

Terrible interface (but lots of content); very expensive for heavy users.

	# of Users	800#	Pricing	Rating
Microsoft Network	1.3 mil.	386-5550	1 month free, then various plans	@@

Nice layout, but expensive

	# of Users	800#	Pricing	Rating
Prodigy	1.2 mil.	776-3449	$9.95 (5 hrs) + $2.95/hr	@@@

Excellent starting point, but also expensive for heavy users.

Table 7-2 Internet Access Providers

	# of Users	800#	Pricing	Rating
AT&T	.6 mil.	967-5363	Free (5 hrs) + $2.95/hr; $19.95	@

Two plans: 5 hrs plus $2.50/hr. or $19.95 unlimited.

	# of Users	800#	Pricing	Rating
Netcom	.5 mil.	501-8649	$19.95 (unlimited)	@@@

Recommended ISP.

	# of Users	800#	Pricing	Rating
MCI	.2 mil.	950-5555	Free (5 hrs); $19.95	@

Only available through MCI's "One" service.

	# of Users	800#	Pricing	Rating
Sprynet	.15 mil.		$19.95	@@

Owned by CompuServe.

Continued

Table 7-2 Internet Access Providers
Continued

	# of Users	800#	Pricing	Rating
GNN	.15 mil.	819-6112	$14.95/20 hrs	@@
Owned by America Online.				
PSI	< .1 mil.	827-7482	$9/mo for 9 hrs	@
UUNet	< .1 mil.	488-6384	$30/mo for 25 hrs	@

Note: Please contact providers for latest pricing; these rates are subject to change.

Ratings: Best - @@@; Worst - @.

America Online

While AOL has had its problems, the release of its 3.0 software upgrade has put it back in the online ball game. Personally, I prefer direct access, but there are many advantages to using AOL and Prodigy as your initial Internet ramp. It matters little once you're on the Internet, as all of the major services give full Web access.

AOL has the most extensive investment area of the online services, but it'll cost you. Though competitive pressures have already forced America Online to cut prices (its latest is the introduction of a 20/20 plan—20 hours for $19.95), AOL still is at a major disadvantage in pricing. The service has 6.2 million subscribers, though, and expects to surpass 10 million sometime in 1997, according to an optimistic

Chairman Steve Case. This makes it by far the single largest gateway to the Internet.

Tom Lichty, author of *The Official America Online Tour Guide*, says of AOL's financial info, "Unlike television or radio, AOL's market information is available whenever you want it: There's no waiting for the 6 o'clock news or suffering through three stories … Unlike newspapers, AOL's financial news is always current. It's not this morning's news; it's this minute's news. It's current, it's always available, and it's almost free. I wonder if Ted Turner knows about this?"

The main thing keeping subscribers at America Online is content. Several of the largest business magazines and fund companies have their own sites built into AOL. Among magazines, information from *Business Week Online*, *Consumer Reports*, and *Worth* may be found, as well as an area from the television show Nightly Business Report. And 11 different mutual fund companies have areas serving the AOL community.

While the offerings are excellent, AOL's convoluted billing practices make it an unkind place to do business. Unless you like being on edge and watching the clock, I suggest you choose another access provider. AOL's introductory rate is $9.95 for 10 hours, then $2.95 an hour, but this is quickly cut to $9.95 for 5 hours the second month—not nearly enough time. However, AOL may soon review its pricing policies once again, due to customer complaints. But if you like the service and can effectively monitor your time online, there's plenty to make it worthwhile.

Resources for investors, which are found in the AOL *Personal Finance* sector, include the following major areas:

Financial Resources, Stocks & Investing, Mutual Fund Center, Market News, Banking & Brokerage Center, Savings & Retirement, Small Business, Credit/Debt, and Consumer Education. Below, I review the Mutual Fund Center, but there are a couple of other resources I'd like to mention first.

AAII, the American Association of Individual Investors, whose Website is covered later, has a nice educational area within the Stocks & Investing area. AOL beginners, in particular, should consult this area. Also, *Worth Online* provides some decent market commentary. Other than that, you've got to work to find much of the good investing advice.

AOL's Mutual Fund Center

Plenty of the major no-load fund companies have presences here, including Fidelity, Vanguard, Strong, T. Rowe Price, Scudder, Dreyfus, Twentieth Century, Berger, Royce, Kaufman, and Founders. Although only Berger, Founders, and Royce Funds have purchase and exchange capabilities as of this writing, most of the other companies are readying trading functions. T. Rowe Price is about to have trading, as is Vanguard (which already offers account viewing). Over the coming months, many of the remaining groups should add account access and trading as well. (DST Systems is providing the trade accounting.)

The Mutual Fund Resource Center on America Online

Run by Jim Lowell, personal finance author and former editor of *FundsNet Insight* (which covers no-load mutual fund "networks"), this area contains plenty of interesting information. One highlight, in particular, is the regular chats sessions. Data available under "Resource Center" includes quotes, message boards, and Morningstar performance numbers. Here are the main features:

- *Morningstar Mutual Funds*—Limited information.

- *Business Week OnLine Mutual Fund Center*—Market commentary and stories.

- *Consumer Reports on Mutual Funds*—Helpful guide to fund buying and some other interesting stuff.

- *Decision Point Mutual Fund Center*—Technical analysis and charts.

- *Market News*—Lackluster comments on market action.

- *Nightly Business Report: Mutual Funds*—Lots of articles, portfolios by Jonathan Pond and others. If you like the PBS program, you'll love the AOL site.

- *Real Life's Mutual Fund Mania*—Don't bother.

- *Worth OnLine Fund Focus*—A little thin, but sometimes has interesting commentary.

- *FundWorks Investors Center*—This is the commentary section with the most fund-specific information.

Articles about hot funds, investing in general, and related topics are found here.

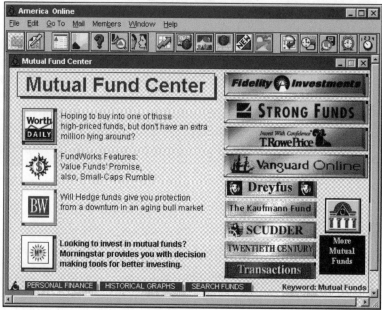

Figure 7-1. AOL's MF Center has everybody who's anybody.

AOL's "Big Four" Fund Groups

The largest and most useful areas may be found in the following sections:

- Fidelity Online Investor Center—This area is practically identical in content to Fidelity's Web site (reviewed in Chapter 10). Features include news and announcements, a fund library with performance (sparse), brokerage services, workplace [401(k) and 403(b)] savings plan information, retirement planning, and a guide to Fidelity.

- Strong—Strong offers some performance and educational materials, and it plans to add account access and trading in the coming months.

- T. Rowe Price—This area allows prospectus downloads, daily fund pricing, performance information, and trading. Also, it includes interviews with fund managers and market updates. This also contains much of the same material as T. Rowe's Website (which is reviewed in Chapter 11).

- Vanguard Online—The Vanguard Group is one of eight fund groups to have set up shop on AOL. Account statements are available online, but it's questionable whether trading will ever come to AOL. The company is reconsidering its plans to proceed with trading here in favor of moving to the Web.

Table 7-3 shows a sample view of the "account value" function within Vanguard's online account access area. (This is a sample IRA account.)

Table 7-3 Sample Vanguard Online Account Values

Fund (acct. #)	NAV	#shares	$ Value
SP ENERGY (09879527922)	$19.12	72.297	$1,382.32
STAR (09879527922)	$15.18	180.648	$2,742.24
IDX-EMGMKT (09879527922)	$11.52	227.060	$2,615.73
	Acct. Value		$6,740.29

Certainly, those of you who've been with AOL for a while should be familiar with many other features, but it would take another book to cover them all. As America Online moves closer to full integration with the World Wide Web, these resources should become more and more synchronized with their Internet counterparts.

The Motley Fool

By now, you may have heard about these guys who ran an investment forum on AOL, or seen their book. As I said in Chapter 6, I think their aggressive stock-picking strategies are downright dangerous. It may be okay for 27-year old computer hackers to be wagering on tech stocks, but buying stocks like Iomega and America Online is ill-advised for most. While they give sound advice on investing in general most of the time, their advice overall is a little too aggressive. Don't be fooled by eye-popping performance numbers. Past performance means nothing in predicting future performance (in investing, anyway). So, read the general educational articles, but stay away from those individual stock model portfolios.

Prodigy

Prodigy, the smallest of the "big three" online services, has a full-featured "Business and Finance" section, which includes plenty of excellent information. Unfortunately, the fund companies themselves have less of a presence here than on the other services. It matters little, though, because Prodigy gives users full Internet access. This way, they may visit the fund group's sites directly. Also, the news and market updates are very good. Overall, I'm a fan of the Prodigy service. If you're a novice, it's perhaps the best single choice out there.

Things should improve because the service was sold by IBM and Sears to its manager and outside investor, International Wireless. Also, Prodigy has Prodigy Internet, a direct-access service, which demonstrates Prodigy's lead over the other online services in making the move entirely onto the Internet. Prodigy has been shifting its Business and Finance content onto the Web for well over a year now, so even non-Prodigy users should be able to access some of this information in the near future.

Within the "Business and Finance" area, the best feature is undoubtedly the AP news listings. These stories give one of the best, most up-to-date news overviews available anywhere. (The news here is even better than that available on much of the Web.) There are also "chats" and market updates, both of which often have informed and concise commentary.

Many of the large fund groups, like Fidelity Investments, have presences on Prodigy as well, but these areas are mere shadows of these funds' AOL setups. As fund companies concentrate more and more on their own Websites, expect their Prodigy sections to wither.

CompuServe

The second-largest online service is a little light as far as fund resources go. It does have a few items of interest, if you

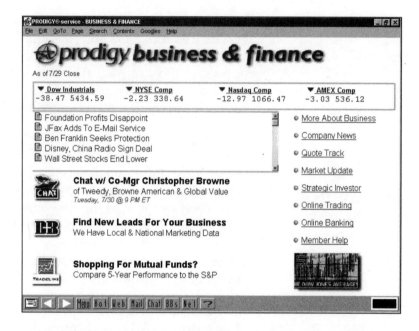

Figure 7-2. The Prodigy service's Business & Finance opening screen.

don't mind hacking your way through layers upon layers of menu screens for each paragraph of text. These include: options for pricing stocks and funds, access to discount brokers online, and more.

One advantage CompuServe does have over its rivals is access to Open Market's OM-Express, software that automatically collects customized information from the Web. Time Warner's Pathfinder (covered in Chapter 9), offers a Personal Edition available free only to CompuServe members, which will allow users to download selected articles from Time Warner publications like *Fortune* and others. Pathfinder Personal Edition is available elsewhere for a monthly fee.

CompuServe, in addition to owning Sprynet, an ISP, has also launched Wow!, a made-for-the-family online service. Wow! has Charles Schwab as its exclusive discount broker, and it has plenty of excellent services. However, unless CompuServe's "Red Dog" transition to the Internet works like a charm, the service will continue fighting an uphill struggle.

Other Specialty BBSs

Finally, there are countless specialized, proprietary bulletin board systems (BBSs), like Fidelity's FOXPro, Reuters' Money Network, and others that allow trading, news gathering, and accessing account information. Some of these may well be merged into Web site development by the companies involved, but I list them here, along with a brief description of some of their features, in case you'd like to investigate them further.

I mention many of these again later within their Web listings, but for now I give one-line summaries of some of the more prevalent packages.

FUND BBSs

While most mutual fund companies don't allow Internet trading yet, many do offer this service via their own online software. The following are several examples:

- Fidelity FOXPro—Fidelity Online Express, which allows online trading of Fidelity funds, as well as access to market information.

127

- Schwab StreetSmart—Allows access to Schwab and online trading with 10 percent discounts.

- Quick & Reilly's QuickWay Plus—Software from the discount brokerage allowing online trading.

- Others—Countless other BBSs are available, but most will fade in importance and use as the Internet becomes the electronic avenue of choice for companies and consumers.

These are just some of the many private online bulletin boards and systems. While I will return to some later, coverage of these areas is beyond the scope of this book.

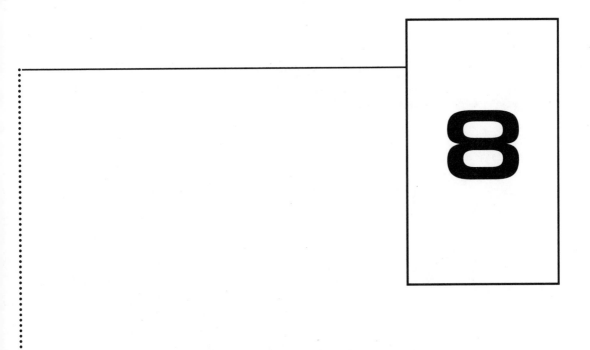

Data and Searching

If you've spent any time whatsoever on the Net, you've probably encountered some of the more popular directories, indexes, or "search engines," such as Yahoo or Digital Equipment Corporation's Alta Vista. These seek out and catalog the 100-million-plus (and counting) Web pages currently in existence. As the Web has grown exponentially over the past five years, the need for cataloging software has exploded. Understandably then, search engine sites are among the most popular sites on the World Wide Web.

This chapter looks at the issues and tools of searches, then reviews each of the major directories and search areas, paying particular attention to those with extensive investment and personal finance listings. Although the sites listed are by no means the only directories and such on the Web, they are the most widely used.

Data: Gotta Have It

By now you've probably realized that finding information on the Web is not a problem, but finding *good* or the *right* information is. These search, rating, and directory sites are the place to start if you're not sure where to begin. A basic search on any one of these services should result in tens, if not hundreds or thousands, of leads.

While these are currently the best of the Net, there are certain to be advances in these technologies in the coming months. Already, customized news services and programs, like Pointcast, Freeloader, and *The Wall Street Journal Interactive Edition*'s Personal Journal, are narrowing the search for useful information even more.

The use of agents and artificial intelligence algorithms is beginning to change the way people search for information. While catalogs like Yahoo and indexes like Magellan and Lycos do a credible job, users need even more sophisticated tools. While they are indeed on the way, for now users must play a game of search hit and miss, as they seek out data.

"Today, the problem is not a lack of information, it's the time it takes to wade through the sources to get what you want," says John Fund, president of Mercury Mail. Mercury Mail's service, Closing Bell, provides daily e-mails of closing stock prices (more on this in Chapter 9). Custom delivery services such as this are one way to cut through the clutter of information.

One solution to this has been "offline" services, like Individual Inc.'s Freeloader, Traveling Software's WebEx (formerly Milktruck), and Forefront Group's Blue Squirrel, that download sites at off-peak times (i.e., in the middle of the night). These types of technologies are expected to be included in the next generation of Web browsers, and they should ease some of the overload during peak times. Browsing offline may be helpful to those who don't have continuous Internet access, but it still doesn't solve the problem of finding the right information.

Search Engines

Without further ado, here are the major search sites currently available on the World Wide Web. These, too, are constantly evolving and rearranging their information directories, so the following information may change. However, the principles behind the types of searches and the methods of searching will be reasonably similar.

When entering a word or phrase to search for, surround it in quotes in order to look for the entire phrase only, put "+" between terms to look for X and Y, and put "-" to exclude (X not Y). Check each site for its specific search directions, though, because some have their own systems.

✳ Yahoo www.yahoo.com

This search site, perhaps the second most famous on the entire Web (after Netscape's HomePage), has seen its traffic grow to almost one million "hits" per day. Its searching capabilities are now powered by Digital's Alta Vista engine, which is discussed later. Yahoo stores other sites by category and displays both a summary and a link with each site. The company was founded by Stanford grad students Jerry Yang and David Filo, who became millionaires in the mania surrounding Internet IPOs in mid-1996.

Yahoo's system is catalogued by category. It starts with the broadest heading: Business and Economy. Users may then move to subcategories, such as Markets and Investments. These are divided even further, with specific Mutual Funds listings available one level deeper. Overall, Yahoo is an excellent resource, though sometimes its random categorization of various sites may make you wonder if just one big category listing wouldn't be preferable.

✳ Alta Vista www.altavista.com

This search engine, designed by Digital Equipment to demonstrate the power of its Alpha servers, competes with HotBot as the most extensive on the Web. It can probably claim the title of fastest engine on the Net and covers over 50 million pages. It catalogs individual pages, rather than entire Web sites, and it includes all Usenet discussion groups. The Yahoo site includes Alta Vista as its engine of choice, making Alta Vista the most popular search engine on the Web.

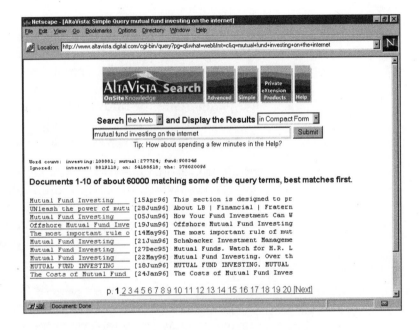

Figure 8-1. Digital's Alta Vista raised the bar for search engines.

Its site states, "AltaVista gives you access to the largest Web index: 30 million pages found on 275,600 servers, and 3 million articles from 14,000 Usenet news groups. It is accessed over 16 million times per weekday." While its reach is exhaustive, Alta Vista's directions for entering search criteria leave something to be desired. I hope, though, that this will improve in future revamps of the site.

✳ HotBot (HotWired & Inktomi) www.hotbot.com

Another "brute force" search engine, which catalogs practically the entire Web, is HotWired and Inktomi's HotBot. This engine, claim its creators, will search every last Web page in existence. By the demonstration searches I've performed, it appears they weren't kidding. I consider HotBot the premier site for finding anything, and I recommend it over Alta Vista for most really tough tasks. For routine tasks, though, Alta Vista gives a generally cleaner listing.

HotBot relies on a network of smaller computers to conduct its searches, which makes it more fault tolerant and faster than those using large machines. It allows for personalized and specialized queries, which are often needed on the larger search engines in order to save you from getting back tens of thousands of responses.

Spokesperson Kevin Brown says of HotBot, "If you put up a page yesterday, there will be a one in seven chance it's in our index today…. By the end of the week, it will be there." HotWired is the online venture of *Wired* magazine; Inktomi is a Berkeley, California, software company.

✳ Excite www.excite.com

Excite is a very well-done resource that reviews sites and lists the review of each site found. Its initial page has a

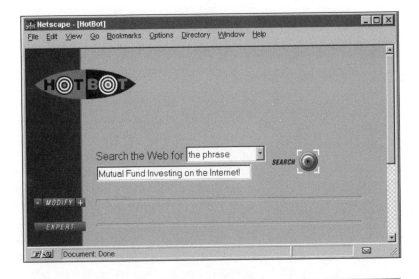

Figure 8-2. Hotbot surpasses Alta Vista as the most extensive search engine.

search option, a directory of reviews, plus news and reference sections. Search options include a general Web search, a search of Excite reviews, or a search of Usenet newsgroups or classifieds. One nice feature is this site's "search for related Web documents" option, which automatically enters the news headline or topic you're viewing into the search engine.

If you're not searching for anything specific, I suggest moving into the Review section's Money area, then entering the Money & Investing subsection for a list of decent investing and personal finance resources. Overall, Excite is an excellent starting point for either searching or browsing listings. Keep in mind that any search is only as intelligent as its data input, so try to narrow down your intent first.

✳ Lycos www.lycos.com
& ✳ Point www.point.com

Lycos's Website consists of the *Lycos* search engine, *A2Z* directory of favorites, and *Point* "top 5 percent of the Web" reviews. The best thing about Lycos is that it screens out most sites, listing only those that have heavy traffic or pass through an editorial staff. It catalogs pages instead of entire sites, providing you with outlines and abstracts for each match of your search criteria.

The site, like Excite, offers both a search and a browse by subject option, as well as a "find related sites" function. Reviews are written by staff and not entered by site submissions. Overall, Lycos makes an excellent starting point, but I prefer Excite slightly.

Within the "Browse by Subject" option, Business/Finance and then Investing and Investments is the section that houses most of the mutual fund resources. The two most useful are Investment Research Resources and Stocks, Bonds, and Mutual Funds.

Netcarta Webmaps

Another feature that appears to be spreading across the Web is the addition of Netcarta Webmaps, which give graphical overviews of sites that have been "mapped" (you need the CyberPilot Pro or another viewer in order to see these though). This allows users to get a quick overview of a site without loading the entire page into the PC.

Expect other software products such as this to be introduced. These products will examine sites and allow users to jump directly to an inside page instead of having to move through each layer of the HomePage.

✳ Infoseek www.infoseek.com

Infoseek's home page offers the Infoseek Guide, which shows pages that match your search criteria, and it also provides lists of pages in related categories, as well as Infoseek Personal, a news customization service. Search universe options include WWW, Infoseek Select sites, Usenet, a company directory, and an e-mail search.

The Business and Finance section is where to look for potential investment sites, but it is rather sparse compared to its competitors. Finally, Infoseek's iZone area features selected "sites of the day." Overall, you're better off starting elsewhere.

✳ Open Text index.opentext.net

Yet another site to begin a search of the Web is Toronto-based Open Text Corp., which like most others offers search, browse, and other functions. While this site doesn't have many of the bells and whistles of its competitors, it does the job as far as searches go. Nonetheless, again I'd suggest sticking with the previous entries as starting points, then trying Open Text if you can't find the information you seek elsewhere.

✳ Web Crawler webcrawler.com

The Webcrawler engine, run by AOL's Global Network Navigator division, does a nice job of organizing retrieved

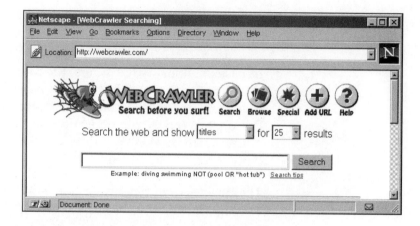

Figure 8-3. Webcrawler is a nicely done search page.

listings. Its Webcrawler Select lists only the "best" sites, which are chosen by its editorial staff. You might want to move right into the Personal Finance section of the directory, which lists almost 20 different subtopics, including Investors' Reference, News and Resources, and Mutual Funds choices.

Ratings Sites

✳ Magellan www.mckinley.com

Magellan reviews and rates World Wide Web sites, providing a short summary and link to a full review. Though

Magellan gets its site descriptions directly from the sites themselves, its editorial staff is one of the best. Magellan's parent, The McKinley Group of Sausalito, California, has merged with Excite Corp., parent of the Excite Guide (reviewed earlier). While it remains to be seen whether these two sites will be fully or only partially integrated, it's clear that the new Excite will be a major player in the search and directory field. Magellan's site is very well done; I recommend it highly for browsing.

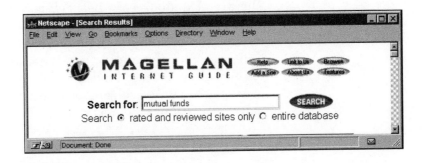

Figure 8-4. McKinley's Magellan Internet Guide.

On the company's mission, Chairman David Hayden says, "McKinley offers ease of use and editorial expertise to rescue Internet users from information overload and guide them to the top sites and resources. The Magellan Finder service is one of these resources, providing users with quick, accurate telephone and e-mail listings on the Web."

Other Search and Ratings Sites

Here are the three final places to begin an information search. While not as widely used as the previous sites listed, each of these has its merits.

```
Search.com (www.search.com)
InfoSpace (www.infospace.com)
Starting Point (www.stpt.com)
```

There will undoubtedly be new, faster, and more refined search functions and sights appearing. But for now, these should be more than enough to find at least some information on anything you could possibly think of. And, as you'll see as we visit more sites, the search engines have news, the news pages have search engines, and each category is gradually merging into the next.

9

News, Online Publications, and Information

If you've been on the Web, you've undoubtedly encountered at least some of the major news outlets. News stories are one of the biggest draws, and promises, of the Internet. But getting up-to-the-minute, well-edited stories remains problematic, particularly on mutual funds and investing. Although there is a flood of information, all too much of it is shabby and half-rate. Much of it is too old, and it takes too long to find the good stuff. This is why I suggest sticking with the giant news media; they're more current and, most importantly, you know where to find them.

News sources are one of the best entertainment features of the Web, and it's now possible to quickly and easily scan and filter through a host of excellent sources, most of which are free, or at least far cheaper than their paper counterparts. This chapter reviews the biggest and the best—the major newspapers' and wire services' sites, TV stations' and magazines' sites, plus several newer "online media" sites.

The New News Media

Everyone in the media business, from local TV stations to Time Warner, has embraced the World Wide Web, not out of promise but out of fear. As cable executive Lee deBoer said in an AP Online story, "All the signs are the Internet will be a powerful force ... in media for a long time." So, they've come—newspapers, television stations, magazines, and a host of newly emboldened competitors and individuals—to compete in the new medium.

The number of news and information providers on the Web is still increasing, but most of the major players have been online for well over a year now. In the fierce new regime of news media on the Internet, the dominant high-end investment sellers—Reuters, Bloomberg, and Dow Jones' Telerate—are going to feel the most pain. For the dominant news outlets, the Internet isn't a matter of making money; it's a matter of survival—trying not to lose too much money as millions of tiny competitors chew away at the edges.

Already some experiments with charging for premium services on the Web are being reconsidered, or at least reduced somewhat. While it remains to be seen whether free or cheap Internet information will seriously threaten the survival of the news giants, it's clear that huge changes are afoot. Some outlets are experimenting with charging fees and with "premium-service" users, but the jury's still out on whether these can make money.

There's so much news out there, in many cases, that your primary consideration is what's the fastest "update spot." You'll want to visit a lot of sites, depending on your information needs, but is chapter gives you a few excellent starting points. These Websites are chosen primarily for their mutual fund and investment news content, but many also cover news topics of general interest as well. Again, any book covering these areas can't possibly remain up-to-date with the newest sites and features, so inconsistencies are inevitable.

As I said (repeatedly in the section on investing), you shouldn't be hinging your investment decisions on news anyway. Even though it's important to be aware of broader trends in society and the economy, an investment decision should be almost oblivious to the daily gyrations of individual companies. With the dawn of instant information and news on the Internet, the challenge has become, as John Bogle is fond of saying, "staying the course." But it's fun and exciting to check out the day's news, and many of these news sites have extensive and excellent investment news stories. A well-informed investor is a wise investor.

As mentioned, any print medium is at an extreme disadvantage regarding sources and description of Websites. The following pages include only the biggest and the best, so I recommend you patronize them. Though an individual Website may have changed since publication of this book, it will probably have only gotten better. Please disregard any antiquated commentary of mine.

Contrary to popular opinion, I believe that the Internet will make large brand names even more important as the consumer becomes bewildered by choices. Newspaper sites, which have the advantage of their extensive libraries of content, are first. Though the television news outlets may catch up once video becomes prevalent on the Web, for now print is still king. The financial TV news sites—CNNfn and CNBC/MSNBC, among others—are next, followed by the magazine and other sites. The chapter finishes with a look at some of the new news "agents" being developed.

❋ Wall Street Journal Interactive Edition wsj.com

Content 📖📖📖📖📖 *Presentation* ☺☺☺☺ *Overall* 💧💧💧💧

Type of info: Business News
Updated: 8:15 a.m., throughout day
Visit: Daily

Comments: The best newspaper in the world runs the best news Website in the world.

This site is a must for any serious investor (or even serious person, for that matter). It's my number one visit when I log onto the Net; the weekend edition's "cyber-column," in particular, is a must read for electronic investors. However, *WSJ Interactive Edition* costs money. It's $29 per year for subscribers to the hardcopy *WSJ*, and $49 per year for non-subscribers. Money extremely well spent, I'd say.

Launched in late April 1996, *wsj.com* passed the 500,000 mark in readership that July. During its free introductory period, the site averaged thousands of new registrations a day. In its free trial period, it was classified as the most heavily traveled business sight on the Internet, and it remains one of the most heavily trafficked.

Figure 9-1. Front page *of The Wall Street Journal Interactive Edition.*

In addition to the entire text of *The Wall Street Journal*, stories are provided by Dow Jones Business Information Services, Dow Jones' electronic publishing unit, plus the *WSJ* international editions (*WSJ* Europe and the Asian *WSJ*) and Dow Jones' News Retrieval.

Personal Journal (a menu choice of the main page), in particular, represents the promise of the Web. You enter several keywords, and you then get news stories tailored. Even though the amount of news can be overwhelming, it's worth it to be able to scan a list of customized stories. The setup of the rest, as you can see from Figure 9-1, is similar to the paper *Journal* (except, of course, for the addition of Sports in the *Interactive Edition.*). I recommend sticking with the Front Page, maybe even for your home page, and checking the Money and Marketplace from there. (Yes, the editorials are there, too. But you don't *have* to read them...)

Other features of the *Journal* include fund and stock quotes (with a "personal portfolio" customized list feature), company "Snapshots," market statistics, and more. It contains over 50,000 pages of information in all, with more being added by the day. It's a must for the serious business cybernaut. (It's also free to users of Microsoft IE 3.0 until the end of 1996.)

✳ USA Today—Money News
www.usatoday.com/money

Content 📖📖📖📖 *Presentation* ☺☺☺☺ *Overall* 💧💧💧

Type/Amount of info: Business, Fund News
Updated: Morning (not frequenly during day)

Comments: A great site, but not as timely as others. For novice investors, it's #1.

As you would expect, *USA Today*'s Website is very friendly and graphically appealing. There's much more information here than in the print version, and I recommend it as *the* daily update spot for beginners. The Money section has three main subsections: Markets, Mutuals, and Spotlight.

Markets contains tons of great stuff. One of my favorites is a daily mutual fund pricing menu option where investors may choose lists of the largest funds' (by type) and of the largest fund families' pricing and performance information. The Markets area also has daily Treasury and bank yields and rates, international market updates and Wall Street commentary. Rate information from Bank Rate Monitor (mentioned in Chapter 13) and news from Data Broadcasting Corp. (mentioned later in Chapter 9) add to the rich selection.

Mutuals has yet more performance data and linked stories on mutual funds, while Spotlight is the "story of the day." Columnists John Waggoner on mutual funds and Kevin Maney on technology are featured; overall they've struck an excellent blend of personal finance and business. The mutual fund information is among the most user-friendly and extensive available on the Internet. I recommend visiting early and often.

☀ *NY Times* on the Web www.nytimes.com

Content 📖📖   *Presentation* ☺☺☺   *Overall* 🖋🖋

Type/Amount of info: Good, but limited
Updated: Early a.m., infrequently during day

Comments: Wait for someone to tell you there's a good article there.

The business section of *The New York Times'* does have the excellent articles for which its paper edition is so well known, including very strong Sunday mutual fund coverage. But the electronic edition adds little to the formula. I'm sure this will change in the future, but until then I suggest looking elsewhere. It is quite convenient though for surfers who prefer the *Times* for their overall daily news.

Features include well-written business stories and great overall corporate coverage, plus quotes galore and other goodies. Its investment and personal finance content is weak during the week. One excellent and growing feature is Rich Meislin's Business Connections: "A selective guide to Internet business, financial, and investing resources"—that is, link city. The quotes have nice search features, plus leader and laggards by fund category options. Finally, the *NYT* layout is very nice.

✳ Investor's Business Daily www.ibd.com

Content 📖📖 *Presentation* ☺☺☺ *Overall* 👍👍👍

Type/Amount of info: Caters to technical investors.
Updated: Throughout day

IBD has entered the daily news-site competition strongly, but I'm not a fan of the paper's "technical-analysis" bent. Nonetheless, the area is well done; the news on business overall is very thorough, and the technology of *Investors Business Daily* is state-of-the-art. Much of the site requires registration, and, as at a lot of other sites, the pricing is yet-to-be determined.

✳ CNN Financial Network (CNNfn)
www.cnnfn.com

Content 📖📖📖📖 *Presentation* ☺☺☺ *Overall* 👍👍👍👍

*Type/Amount of info: Plenty of good business and finance news
Updated: Semi-continuously*

Comment: Parent CNN keeps its news backlog well stocked.

This site also gives an excellent news wrap-up. As all of these news areas advance in speed and graphical capabilities, there may not be any need for the "paper" paper anymore. CNNfn, however, has left something to be desired in the prompt update department. Features include Grapevine (rumor of the day), Interact, Managing Money/Business, Markets (quotes, data, economic stories), News, Programs, Resources (company sites, tax info, general reference, and more).

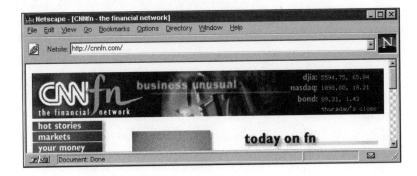

Figure 9-2. CNNfn may be behind CNBC on TV, but it's taken the lead on the Web.

CNNfn, or *fn*, as it is beginning to be referred to as, has links with Pathfinder, parent Time Warner's (or rather Time Warner Turner's) massive site (listed later, along with publications *Money* and *Fortune*).

✳ MSNBC www.msnbc.com

Content 📖📖📖 *Presentation* ☺☺☺☺ *Overall* 👍👍👍

Type/Amount of info: Limited but good in-depth articles
Updated: Regularly

Comment: Good in-depth stories, but no real-time news.

This site, in addition to having business and finance stories in its Commerce section, also hosts CNBC's, the financial news network's, site within its borders. The articles have been excellent here, though for breadth of news it leaves something to be desired. Parent MSNBC's Front Page general news gives it a big advantage, though. Look for this area to become a player in the investment news area on the Web.

✳ CNBC www.cnbc.com

Content 📖 *Presentation* ☺☺☺ *Overall* 👍👍

Type/Amount of info: Terminology for beginners
Updated: Once a day

Comments: Skeletal content.

This site, reflective of its TV parent, features discussion and personal finance. Although sparse at first, they should be adding content; its features include *The Squawk Box* and *The Money Club*.

☀ Bloomberg www.bloomberg.com

Content 📖📖📖📖 *Presentation* ☺☺ *Overall* 👓👓👓👓

Type/Amount of info: Tons of stories, but short takes
Updated: All the time

Comments: Plenty of stories, but in-depth versions are reserved for paying customers.

Bloomberg, which makes the famed news "boxes" prevalent in securities firms (and other places wealthy enough to afford their thousand-dolla-a-month cost), has entered the Internet news business forcefully. Its pages aren't the most technically sophisticated, but, boy does it have the news.

Bloomberg's mutual fund news page alone is enough to keep you reading for days, and the stories are distributed rapidly (not long after appearing on the boxes).

Other News Sources of Note

The following sites are merely mentioned here. You'll undoubtedly become familiar with many other options as the competition between news providers shakes out.

Reuters

www.reuters.com

The giant of international news has moved onto the Web to protect its turf. Definitely take advantage of its free sections. The news is updated frequently, and the coverage is extenive. A very nice index may be found here.

DBC Online's Newsroom

(www.dbc.com)

I look at this Website in Chapter 13, but it deserves mention here, too. It provides selected news stories, quotes, and services for many of the larger news sites, and it is one of the very few "real-time" news providers (for free!) on the Net.

Iguide

This "Internet directory" run by Rupert Murdoch's NewsCorp., is a very well-done, all-around resource. Its reviews are nice, and the index structure is easy to follow. (The Money area is at:
http://www.iguide.com/work_mny/index.sml).

LeadStory

(www.leadstory.com)

AT&T's "story of the day" does what it says. This is an excellent site.

Local News Sources

Though I won't list all of them here, plenty of local news organizations and papers have sites with investing news. Many of these are now using the Associated Press (AP)'s WIRE Web service, so they have excellent news. Here is just a tiny sampling:

The Washington Post

(washingtonpost.com)

Look here for political stories.

The Boston Globe's Business

(boston.com)

I'm a little partial to this local site, but what the heck. The *Globe* has plenty of good fund information, and it often has very good stories on Fidelity and other mutual funds.

San Jose Mercury News' Mercury Center

(www.sjmercury.com)

This paper specializes in technology news. It also pioneered Mercury Center, a subscription product. (The headlines are free, but access to full stories is currently $4.95 a month.)

Customized News Sources

Another news source that you'll likely encounter on the pages above and elsewhere is the "personalized news service." These companies take a user profile and either e-mail or allow users access to stories that are tailored to their interests.

Closing Bell by Mercury Mail

This free service (www.merc.com or e-mail to signup@merc.com) provides daily summaries of closing prices (by 6:45 p.m.) and market summaries.

Individual, Inc.'s NewsPage

(www.newspage.com)

This company offers customized news delivery, for a fee; it also has plenty of free news resources at its site.

PointCast Network

This service, prevalent on inactive PC screens, reached its 1996 goal of a million viewers in only five months and is still growing at a rate of 250,000 new viewers per month. Its Cupertino, California, broadcasting center receives more than 35 million hits each day!

IBM's InfoSage

(www.infosage.ibm.com)

This is another advanced customized news source that takes advantage of agents and advanced search technology. Almost everything here, however, will cost you substantially.

Magazines

Almost every print publication has come out with its own electronic version, but the quality of these varies widely. Although

I cover only the largest and best, thousands of specialized publications are available to help with specific questions.

✳ Barron's Magazine Online
www.barrons.com

Content 📖📖📖 *Presentation* ☺☺ *Overall* 👍👍👍

Type/Amount of info: For serious investors (and readers!) Updated Saturday 8 a.m.

Comments: Excellent for hardcore investors and if you like the magazine.

Unveiled in July 1996, this site contains all of the in-depth (and skeptical) articles that *Barron's* is so well known for, and more. Columnist Thomas G. Donlan summed the weekly's mission up nicely in the pioneer electronic edition, saying, "The editors of *Barron's* believe that the new medium will add to *Barron's* 75-year tradition of putting professional-strength information in the hands of individual investors."

In addition to its excellent editorial content, the *Barron's* page offers access to both company and mutual fund "dossiers." These reports include NAVs, dividends, yields, latest distribution, news links (both *Barron's* articles and general news), and performance views. The latter contain charts, which unfortunately weren't adjusted for distributions.

All of the statistics in the paper *Barron's* MarketWeek section aren't yet available, but they should be in the coming months.

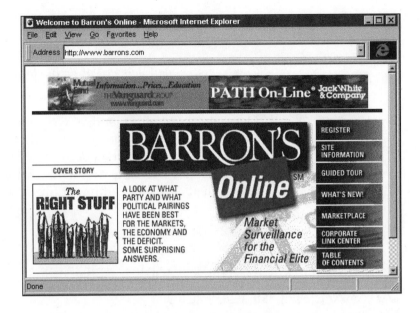

Figure 9-3. *Barron's* site is state of the art, including frames, links galore, and an extensive database.

Future plans include Investor Workstation, a premium service that allows sophisticated charting and screening techniques on companies, funds, and market indexes. For example, investors may chart a stock's earnings growth against others in its industry.

✳ Money Magazine Online
www.pathfinder.com

Content 📖📖📖 *Presentation* ☺☺ *Overall* 👍👍

Type/Amount of info: Business stories
Updated: Evenings

Comments: E-mail delivery of daily story and market stats is a nice feature.

Money's site contains plenty of well-written business and personal finance stories. One nice feature is automatic e-mail of the daily story and market summary. Finally, *Money Online's* bulletin board has daily discussions. However, most interactive content is within Pathfinder (described next).

✳ Pathfinder (Fortune, Other Time Inc.) www.pathfinder.com

Content 📖📖📖 *Presentation* ☺☺☺☺☺ *Overall* 👍👍👍👍

Type/Amount of info: Business stories and news
Updated: Evenings

Other Time Warner publications may also be found at the Pathfinder site. These sometimes have mutual fund articles; besides the aforementioned *Money*, publications include.

Fortune, the weekly business magazine (not much fund info), *Time Magazine* and more.

Pathfinder Personal Edition

This premium service allows users to pick articles from a selection of publications, providing a customized news-magazine.

✳ Mutual Funds Magazine Online www.mfmag.com

Content 📖📖 *Presentation* ☺ *Overall* 👍👍

Type/Amount of info: Nothing but mutual funds, but better info is available elsewhere
Updated: Daily

Mutual Funds Magazine, a publication launched by newsletter writer Norman Fosback, was on the Net early, putting a large investment into the new technology. It's paid off because not only is the MF site very helpful, but its alerts and mailings are also state-of-the-art. It's definitely worth a visit, though I wouldn't advise buying anything.

Charter memberships to the site are currently $4.99 per month. Although I advise against spending this much, the service does offer some features that aren't widely available elsewhere, such as sophisticated fund screening tools.

✳ Worth Online www.worth.com

Content 📖📖📖 *Presentation* ☺☺☺☺ *Overall* 👍👍👍

Type/Amount of info: Business stories
Updated: Evenings

The magazine's online counterpart has come from nowhere with a strong showing. It has a bunch of features, including the famed Peter Lynch's column, searches, message boards,

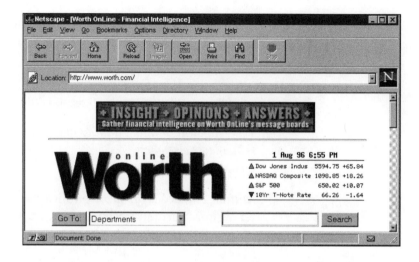

Figure 9-4. New entrant *Worth* intends to save flagging newstand sales.

a newsletter, and more. This site is certainly worth browsing on occasion.

✻ Kiplinger's Magazine www.kiplinger.com

Content 📖📖📖 *Presentation* ☺☺ *Overall* 👍👍👍

Type/Amount of info: Use for personal finance and fund articles
Updated: Daily

The *Kiplinge's* site is a nice offering with access to both the magazine's personal finance and mutual fund stories, plus the expert tax advice of *Kiplinger's* other publications.

Other Magazines Online

✳ *Forbes Magazine* www.forbes.com

✳ *Research Magazine* Online www.researchmag.com/8

✳ *U.S. News* Online www.usnews.com

✳ *Green Magazine* members.aol.com/greenzine/INDEX.1.HTM

Premium Data Services and Other Media

Though I'm concentrating on services for individual investors, you should know that there are a host of premium data sellers and services available. Certainly for financial market professionals, the options available and the amount of information will only continue to explode. The Internet may be driving prices down across the board, but it hasn't exactly put some of these providers out of business.

Most of them have been represented either above or in the coming chapters. They have no choice but to compete with, and on, the Internet.

Part IV

Mutual Fund Company
Web Sites

Chapters 10 through 14 make up the meat of the book—mutual fund, discount broker, investment information, and personal finance Web sites. I tell you where they're located and give a brief overview of what's on them, which ones to visit, how much time to spend there, and where to find specific investment information on each. Omitted are some sites that focus primarily on individual stocks, but the line had to be drawn somewhere. But most of the larger stock-picker's sites are at least mentioned.

Since mutual funds have become omnipresent in the investment world, it's rare to find a company or information provider that doesn't at least peripherally address funds. However, the more aggressive the site's investing philosophy, the less coverage is devoted to it here. Short-term and technical speculation on individual stocks has no place among the sane person's investments. (They should be covered in the work, "Gambling on the Internet.") Nonetheless, you'll certainly see your share of aggressive tactics among the Websites we'll visit. Mutual funds see their share of speculation too.

In Chapter 10, I critique the "Big 3" of the no-load investment world—Fidelity Investments, Charles Schwab & Co., and The Vanguard Group, all of which have extensive Web sites. Their home pages clearly not only are catering to their own investors and retirement plan participants, but are built with the idea of marketing to new potential investors. They do this, of course, by making the sites helpful and informative to everyone. They are also in the forefront of Internet site technology, and they set the standards for both content and presentation as far as fund company Websites go.

These three companies alone have thousands upon thousands of pages of information on mutual funds and investing, so I will cover their online offerings most extensively. By exploring these areas in depth, you'll not only further familiarize yourself with mutual funds and investing strategies but you'll also have an excellent idea of the features and information available on most other fund groups' sites. Even investors in other fund groups will be able to take advantage of the extensive resources here.

Chapter 11 covers most of the remaining significant no-load fund sites. Particular attention is devoted to such "mega-sites" as Galt Technologies' NETWorth, which contains dozens of different fund families. Fund groups covered in this chapter include: T. Rowe Price, Twentieth Century/Benham, Dreyfus, Scudder, Invesco, Stein Roe, Strong, and more. Plus, NETWorth's site has sections for IAI, Safeco, Montgomery, and many others. (Both Fidelity and Vanguard may be adding links to NETWorth in the near future.)

Even though the no-load groups are my main focus, I include brief descriptions of current "load" and bank-sponsored fund sites as well. Some of these areas have excellent personal finance resources and investment news features as well. Because the World Wide Web is the ultimate place for do-it-yourselfers, I thought it appropriate to stick with no-loads. Also, most of the broker and advisor funds have little incentive to attempt to sell from the Internet, so they're severely underrepresented there.

Next, Chapter 12 looks at the discount brokers' sites, where for now anyway, the bulk of the live Internet trading is taking place. While these companies' sites are used primarily for individual stocks, most deal heavily in funds as well and have fund network programs. Jack White and the PAWWS Financial Network, E*Trade, Lombard Securities, Quick & Reilly, and more are reviewed here; each of these has "fund network" capabilities where investors may purchase no-load funds from a variety of families.

Although purchasing some funds through these networks will result in an additional charge, I point out those with the most favorable "no-transaction-fee" programs. I also spell out why, in most cases, "no transaction" doesn't necessarily mean no transaction, and thus why investors are better off sticking directly with the fund families themselves. This chapter ends with a brief mention of full service brokerage sites, such as Merrill Lynch and Prudential Securities. The biggest of these companies are moving to the Web forcefully to counter the onslaught of new competition.

10

The Big 3—
Fidelity, Schwab, and Vanguard

Thousands of mutual funds (over 7,000 at last count) and hundreds of fund companies are vying for investors' business. The number of funds and fund groups continues to grow, leaving investors with a truly bewildering number of choices. This is the case today, but experts have predicted that within the next decade the number of fund companies (and funds) will be cut in half. No, you don't have to worry about your money disappearing, but you do have to worry about the smaller players' Web sites disappearing.

More importantly, as competitive pressures build, you will have to be concerned about smaller companies raising their fees to stay profitable. This (cost) is but one reason that I suggest sticking with the giants; the other reasons are convenience, variety, service, and, most importantly, the added degree of insurance they offer merely because they are big.

On the other hand, the bigger players will be forced to stick it out, even should their Websites remain a drag on their profitability. Smaller fund companies will have a tough time spending the money it takes to stay on the cutting edge of the Internet, especially when it comes to online trading and account maintenance. T. Rowe Price's Mark Mitchell was quoted by *Fund Action*, an industry newsletter, saying "Everyone is struggling with what is the value [of a Web site]." Thus, I predict that the Web will accelerate the consolidation trend within the fund industry.

Although the continued growth of the fund industry has allowed marginal players to survive and has even allowed anyone with an idea (and a garage) to start up their own fund, this will change during the first market downturn. Already, the giants are capturing a larger and larger share of new money flowing into funds. This is one of the reasons why these three companies in particular are featured so prominently—most of you will already have accounts at one of them.

Clearly, the major no-load companies are taking advantage of the new communications channel. But this is only the beginning. The Web holds promise for these companies like no other industry due to their information- and transaction-intensive nature. They are leading the way and setting precedents like no other companies online. Whereas before it was prohibitively expensive to direct shareholders and potential shareholders to the educational information that would assist them in making a proper investment decision, the Web makes this possible—and inexpensive.

New Vanguard Group Chairman John J. Brennan says, "We believe that the online medium has the potential to revolutionize shareholder service in the same manner that the toll-free 800 telephone number has over the past 15 years." If the no-load fund groups and discount brokerages master the Internet in the way they mastered the 800-number medium, it will only be a matter of time before they're moving into the banking and insurance industries' turf.

✳ Fidelity Investments www.fid-inv.com

No-Load Mutual Fund Family
800/544-8888 Boston, Massachusetts

Content 📖📖📖 *Presentation* ☺☺☺☺ *Overall* 👍👍👍

Time You Should Spend ☺☺
Don't Miss Feature-Fund Perspectives on Performance
Strength—Profiles on individual funds, articles
Weakness—Little news, market statistics

Site Statistics: Over 3,000 pages of info; over 100,000 "hits" a day at its site

Fund Family Statistics: Assets—$415+ billion; Funds—237; Other— First to offer money funds

NAVs: Updated after 7pm
News: Yes, but slim

Educational Stuff: Extensive

Fund Performance Numbers: Dated but extensive; 1-yr; 3-yr; 5-yr #'s; nice format

Special Deals: MCI Internet access offer ($17.95/month for 20 hrs + $1.95/hr)

Fidelity investors may find plenty to do at this site, but most other readers will probably want to limit their time here. At least, that is, until Fidelity wises up and starts directing some of its massive internal research and market news/data budget toward Webgoers. The information and news available at its site is downright sparse, given Fidelity's extensive resources. (Estimates are that Fidelity is spending upward of $2 million a year on its site.) See Figure 10-1.

Figure 10-1. Fidelity Investments' Home Page. This pretty much says it, but check out the fund profiles.

Certainly, the addition of @82DEV, a financial news area, has alleviated this somewhat. It takes the place of Fidelity's NewsWorthy section and consists of some market news, personal finance and investing articles, and more. The offerings are sparse now, but Fidelity has been continuously updating each area; this approach is an example of the *kaizen*, or constant improvement, philosophy of chairman/owner Edward "Ned" Johnson III.

Mary Ruth Moran, senior vice presidentof electronic channel development, says, "After ... interacting with customers on the Internet, we've learned quite a bit about their requirements, and we're responding aggressively to keep pace with their demand for more content.... Each time we've added new areas to our site, we've seen a sustained increase in the traffic to our server, which is now tracking more than one million hits per month.... @82DEV will provide investors with a daily dose of investment news and information, giving them even more reasons to keep coming back to Fidelity's Web site."

@82DEV's four main areas are (1) Focus Today—investment and related info; (2) The Hub—market data via Thomson Financial Services' lackluster MarketEdge site (reviewed in Chapter 13); (3) The "F" Files—educational articles; and (4) 02109—news and information about Fidelity. If you can stand the wait while the extensive graphics load, this area adds tremendously to the overall site. I especially like the economic calendar.

Schedules for upcoming Investor Center seminars are available, as are some informative Fidelity publications. Fidelity's description lists its features as "new and noteworthy information such as new funds, products, or services being introduced; upcoming seminars at many of our Investor Centers located nationwide, as well as reprints of some of the most recent articles from a selection of Fidelity publications."

In all fairness, Fidelity does offer a service with extensive resources. Its *RealTime Research* is open to qualified brokerage investors for $5.00 a month, and it has its own home page. This package includes Morningstar Mutual Fund Reports, FundsNetwork Performance Directory, Standard & Poor's Stock Screens, and more. (Call 800/544-3198 to sign up, but only if you're a Fidelity brokerage customer.)

What to Do at the Site

Visit Fund *Perspectives on Performance* (located under the fund data area; it must be downloaded to view with Adobe Acrobat).

Get prospectuses, fund NAVs, performance, and other fund information.

Visit Fidelity's Workplace Savings area, which has plenty of helpful commentary, including its *Stages* magazine.

Fidelity's seven other sections (in addition to @82DEV) are Mutual Fund Library, Investment & Retirement Planning, Brokerage Services, Workplace Savings, Investment Advisors & TPAs, Investor's Guide to Fidelity, and Contests & Games.

Mutual Fund Library

This area is the main attraction. Data galore on Fidelity's mutual funds is here, including objectives, performance history, and fund managers. Electronic prospectuses are available for download (you'll need Adobe's Acrobat Reader to read the PDF files). There is an abundance of information here, especially if you're one of the millions of Fidelity investors—either directly or through 401(k) plans. Prospectuses are available for most funds (Fidelity hopes to have all soon); they're marked by a little document 📖 symbol.

Investment & Retirement Planning

Fidelity gets an A for its collection of educational materials, articles, and interactive investment planners "designed to assist you as you create your own personal mutual fund portfolio, fine-tune an existing portfolio, plan for a child's college educational costs as well as your own retirement." However, if you've seen the paper versions, there's not much new material here.

Brokerage Services

In case you didn't know it, Fidelity, too, has a discount brokerage, as well as its FundsNetwork(R), where hundreds of other families' mutual funds are available (for no fee or a small fee). Bonds may also be purchased. The commissions are very competitive, so Fidelity remains one of the top choices among brokers. Included here are comprehensive lists of Fidelity's different accounts and services.

Workplace Savings

Thousands upon thousands of companies, many of them smaller businesses, have chosen a Fidelity savings option at work. Private companies, through a 401(k) plan, and non-profit organizations or public schools, via 403(b) plans, will find "a selection of educational materials, investment articles, and downloadable worksheets..." Though you won't want to spend all day here, you'll definitely give it a visit, especially if you're a Fidelity investor. Expect this area to get a major share of the sites' developmental resources in the future.

Fidelity NetBenefits

Online trading has come to Fidelity's retirement investors, but only if your company is signed up (and has its plan directly with Fidelity, not with someone else who offers Fidelity funds). Accessed through the Workplace Savings section of Fidelity's Website, everything from checking account balances to placing trades may be done here. This area also includes quotes, indexes, fund performance data, a function for modeling loans or withdrawals and future allocation adjustment options. This is a start, but it's yet to be seen how many of the nation's almost five million 401(k) and 403(b) plan participants with Fidelity funds will be allowed access by their employers. (Let yours know!)

Investor's Guide to Fidelity

As you'd expect, information about Fidelity and how to contact the company is listed here. Describing the different types of accounts and services at Fidelity is an enormous task, but these various pages do a clear and concise job of it. For those interested in opening an account, I'd recommend that you take some time to tour this area.

Investment Advisors' Area

Registered Investment Advisors (RIAs) who sell Fidelity funds will find plenty here. Fidelity's Advisor program has been growing madly in recent years, due mainly to the public's desire for guidance. Fidelity states, "Here, you can learn about a wide range of competitive products backed by cutting-edge technologies and comprehensive support that can help you manage your business more effectively."

Contests & Games

Visit this area to test your investment skills and knowledge and try your hand at winning prizes; guess the Dow. Like most of these areas on the Web, this is merely a guise for getting your data onto a mailing list.

Ordering Literature

Fund prospectuses, applications, and literature will be delivered to you by request (for those items unavailable online). Most fund prospectuses are currently available for downloading directly to your PC, and all should be available in the coming months.

Getting Around Fidelity's Site

Fidelity does a nice job of keeping each page manageable, and it allows for easy navigation with well-placed menus. The introductory page has both graphical and text choices for the eight sections, and options for both search and index make things even easier. Finally, it gives you plenty of chances to give feedback, so I reckon the site will probably undergo major renovations in the near future. (I hope Fidelity will get rid of the obscene red background in @82DEV!)

What Do Other People Think of the Site?

Barron's—"A big, fancy site. Nice graphics, with some downloadable prospectuses, daily NAVs, but outdated portfolio holdings. ... Without account data, though, not worth visiting this or most other fund company pages too often."

Information available on all funds, except money market funds, includes: objective, manager, inception, 1-, 3-, 5-, 10-year and life-of-fund returns, NAVs, fees, loads and minimums, and so on. Also included are the fund's top 10 holdings and top industries. While the amount of data is more than you could ever ask for, it is somewhat dated. However, I hope Fidelity will have moved to daily performance updates across the board by the time this is published. Figure 10-2 shows the layout of the fund data.

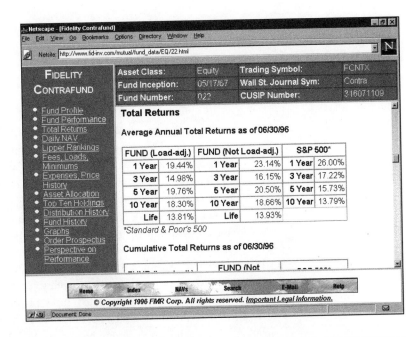

Figure 10-2. Fidelity's fund profiles are absolutely loaded with
information.

In Their Own Words:
Mutual Funds Gradually
Enter the Computer Age

Nearly 70 percent of Fidelity customers own personal computers, and
about three quarters of those are equipped to access the Internet or other
online services. In theory, that group of customers can use their computers to review fund prospectuses, as well as other fund information, and
to buy or sell fund shares through a computer network. In practice, legal
rules and operational constraints have limited the use of computers for
mutual fund investing.

The Securities and Exchange Commission (SEC) recently issued an interpretive release to allow investors easier computer access to mutual fund documents. However, significant legal and operational barriers still exist to the purchase or sale of mutual fund shares through a computer network.

At this time, customers will not be able to use the Internet to purchase or sell shares in a Fidelity mutual fund. This is because Fidelity continues to be concerned about the security of monetary transactions carried out online, given the current state of technology. Nevertheless, Fidelity may run a pilot program on making fund exchanges on the Internet. Fidelity will also closely follow developments in computer security, which in the future may provide adequate protection for online monetary transactions.

In addition, Fidelity hopes to create a system that lets customers use their computers to vote proxies on their Fidelity mutual funds. Mutual fund customers have traditionally voted fund proxies by mail, and more recently by phone. It should be possible to develop software and identification numbers for proxy voting because it does not involve the difficult security issues that monetary transactions do.

In short, mutual funds are gradually entering the computer age. Online customers can now access various fund documents through Fidelity's home page and use that information to purchase or sell funds by mail or phone. As security concerns are resolved through technological advances, Fidelity will try to develop a mechanism for interested customers to effect monetary transactions through a computerized network.

— *Robert C. Pozen, general counsel and managing director (Source: Fidelity's Website)*

In addition to its Website, Fidelity has myriad other options for communications and transactions. Fidelity's On-Line Express (FOX) software is available for $49.95 and allows trading through a user's PC. Also, Fidelity has several automated phone systems, and it has an extensive presence on America Online, Prodigy, and Microsoft Network.

Your first stop should be: *Getting To Know The Fidelity WWW Server*. This may be reached in the Index section off the main menu. You should quickly be able to determine whether the information you're looking for is at this site.

In the mutual fund world, as I've said, Fidelity is *The Empire*, an excellent, all-around financial company. While the stunning performance of its early years may be a thing of the past due to the now tremendous size of its growth funds (Magellan has about $50 billion in assets), the sheer number of fund options and services available makes Fidelity an excellent choice for more active investors.

✳ Charles Schwab & Co. www.schwab.com

No-Load Fund Family/Discount Broker
800/435-4000 San Francisco, California

Content 📖📖📖 *Presentation* ☺☺☺☺ *Overall* 💧💧💧💧

Time You Should Spend There ☺☺☺
Don't Miss Feature-FundSelect Data
Strength—Trading
Weakness—Overwhelming number of fund choices

Site Statistics: Well over 1,500 pages of info
Schwab and FundsNetwork Funds

Fund Family Statistics: Assets—$36+ billion; Funds—24 (only counting Schwab funds)

NAVs: Y (updated at around 6:15 p.m.)
News: Y
Educational Materials: Y

Individual Fund Data: Extensive, but slightly dated
Performance: 3-, 6-mo, 1-, 5-, 10-yr

Technically, this site should be listed with Chapter 12, Discount Brokers, but Schwab has used its dominance in the discount brokerage business to become a force in mutual funds, second only to Fidelity Investments. The company now offers investors the choice of more than 1,100 funds from 150 well-known fund families. Its *FundsNetwork* offers investors "one-stop shopping" where they can trade

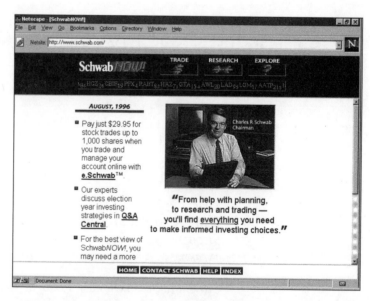

Figure 10-3. Schwab's *OneSource* fund program makes it the best choice for consolidating investments.

hundreds of different funds with no transaction fees, and thousands with a low commission.

Through this program Schwab controls a huge chunk of the mutual fund assets of many smaller no-load companies, such as Berger, Founders, and SteinRoe. It remains to be seen whether Fidelity's recent withdrawal from Schwab's FundsNetwork program will hurt it. But Schwab also keeps adding fund groups, Scudder being the most recent. Schwab has been at the forefront of software and tele-broker technology, so it is no surprise that its Website is impressive. Figure 10-3 shows Schwab's introductory screen.

What to Do at the Site

Try Schwab's demo trading module to practice buying and selling stocks or funds online.

Get prospectuses, fund NAVs, performance and fund information.

Run through Schwab's "Develop an Investment Plan" module (located in the Explore area).

While Schwab's extensive product lineup and world-renowned service make it an excellent one-stop shop for investors, sometimes the number of choices can get you into more trouble than they're worth. It now has four main options for investors: Schwab Funds, Schwab's Mutual Funds *Select List*, Schwab's *OneSource*, and Schwab's entire universe of fund.

Schwab Funds—The company's own proprietary family of funds, these include 24 different funds with 1.8 million shareholders and over $36 billion in assets. These are among the lowest-cost funds, specializing in index and plain-vanilla fund choices. Schwab has also added several asset allocation funds—the Asset Director series, which make excellent starter or "all-in-one" funds for those who want to simplify their lives.

Schwab's Mutual Fund *Select List*—These are funds with at least five years of performance data that Schwab chooses by evaluating their risk versus return. Generally, these funds will include the highest performers. I'd suggest ignoring these funds and choosing according to which fund's strategy best fits your goals, not which has the best performance.

Schwab's OneSource—This includes over 500 no-load, no-transaction fee funds from over 70 fund families. If you can't find the type of fund you want here, you're not looking hard enough.

Schwab's TeleBroker—Making the PC Obsolete?

For those of you who still prefer to use the telephone, Schwab's automated system surpasses most. It has been practicing for over a decade, and often the phone is still the fastest means to buy and sell a stock or to get a quote update.

Schwab customers know the number (800/2-Schwab) for 24-hour access to quotes, account updates, orders, and more. Recently added features include automatic listings of your stocks, dividend reinvestment, fractional shares and yet more funds. There's nothing wrong with your using the phone instead of your computer!

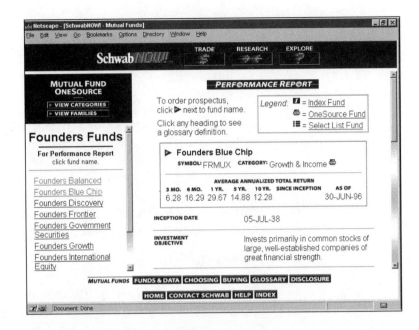

Figure 10-4. Performance data is extensive, even on non-Schwab funds.

As far as performance and other information on individual funds goes, Schwab has done a stellar job. It lists not only plenty of data (though slightly dated), but also gives investors expenses, including 12b-1 (or marketing) fees, objectives, betas (a measure of how closely the fund tracks the market), expenses, minimums, portfolio turnover, and more. (See Figure 10-4.)

Schwab has been on the front edge of the technology boom, but even it was surprised by the speed at which the move to the Web took place. Cheaper, "deep-discount" brokers like E*Trade and eBroker posed a serious threat to Schwab, but the company has responded swiftly and effectively. Schwab's e.Schwab online discount brokerage trading service reduced its commissions to a flat $29.95, which has helped the company gain approximately 50 percent of the online stock trading market. I'll return to the battle of the discount brokers in Chapter 12.

Schwab unveiled its trading on the Web in July 1996. Not only do investors get a 10 percent discount on brokerage commissions (this discount is also available through Schwab's Telebroker phone and Streetsmart software services), but you can get real-time quotes (most others are delayed 15 minutes), historical price charts, and online trading services. Schwab's *e.Schwab* option is discussed below.

e.Schwab

E.Schwab is Charles Schwab's all-electronic trading subsidiary. Stocks, funds, and tons of other securities may be traded for one flat fee. Though the service levels here are mighthy thin, the price is right. If you are going to trade stocks, Schwab's e.Schwab subsidiary is the place to do it.

Schwab's site is ready to cater to traders, giving them both cheap and efficient Web trading, plus access to as much research as you can handle (and can afford, in some cases). Its three choices—Trade, Research, Explore—pretty much sum up the plan. Not just traders, but potential traders and investors of all stripes will find interesting things here.

As far as a presence on other online services goes, for Wow! users, Schwab has an exclusive trading agreement with the new, targeted-at-youth service of CompuServe. Full trading and access to Schwab's Websites are offered here, so customers of Wow!

should check out Schwab's area. (Be sure and check with the companies for the most current fees and trading rates.)

Finally, Schwab has been adding interactive and educational materials to broaden its assault on the entire financial services industry. It looks as if this site's going to be the one to watch for more experienced investors. But everyone should at least check in once in a while to see what Schwab's doing now.

✳ The Vanguard Group www.vanguard.com

No-Load Mutual Fund Family
800/662-2739 Valley Forge, Pennsylvania

Content 📖📖📖📖 *Presentation* ☺☺☺☺☺ *Overall* 👆👆👆👆👆

Time You Should Spend There ⊕⊕⊕⊕
Don't Miss Feature Online University
Strength—Educational material, Fund information/profiles
Weakness—No market/daily news

Site Statistics: Over 1,000 pages of information

Fund Family Statistics: Assets—$415+ billion; Funds—90+; Other—Lowest costs in industry

NAVs: Yes, Updated at 7 p.m.
News: Yes
Educational Materials: Y (Best on the Web)

Fund Performance Numbers: 1-yr; 3-yr; 5-yr; nice format

Known as the most conservative and tight-fisted of fund groups, Vanguard hasn't skimped where its Website is concerned. It remains the best mutual fund company Website, and it has more general investment information than any other single place on the Internet. While it certainly has its share of marketing material, its education section is the first place novice investors should visit on the Web.

In case you haven't figured it out by now, the Vanguard Group, the rebel forces in the battle for dominance of the no-load mutual fund world, is a favorite of mine. Its Website is exceptional, a showcase fund company site. Like Fidelity's site, Vanguard's contains an enormous amount of information, over a thousand pages of content—fund data, investment advice, and more.

Its "Website navigation map" (covered in the following pages) is an excellent touch; it is a hyperlink tour-de-force. Although many of the sites I've seen are adding site maps or indexes for browsers to instantly locate a particular area, Vanguard was the first major fund group with this feature. Figure 10-5 shows the Vanguard Homepage.

What to Do at the Site

Learn about investing, indexing, and types of different mutual funds.

Figure 10-5. Vanguard's site is probably the best educational site out there.

Get prospectuses, fund NAVs, performance and fund information.

Custom Price Report—Select which Vanguard funds you own or would like to monitor, and you'll be able to view an online report containing fund names, NAVs, tickers, inception dates, changes in NAVs, plus year-to-date, 1-, 5- and 10-year total returns.

The site is organized into four main areas: Mutual Funds, Education, Services, and Planning Tools.

Mutual Funds

This section contains all the information you could ever want on any of the 80+ Vanguard funds—each of them "managed for specific objectives, following tightly prescribed strategies, and with relatively predictable investment characteristics." Searches are available alphabetically by name and by category, and fund profiles are easily accessible.

Each *Vanguard Fund Profile* contains comprehensive information on the fund, from investment objective and philosophy to performance and account options. You'll also have the ability to request Fund prospectuses. Each profile consists of four sections. Use the button bar near the top of each profile to navigate through the sections:

1. Objective—This section describes each fund's: Investment Objective and Philosophy; Performance; Fund Services ; Distribution Schedule, etc. It also allows you to download or order a prospectus.

2. Manager(s)—This section is not as important here as at some other fund groups because most Vanguard funds stick closely to their broad indexes or charters.

3. Investment Strategy—This ection outlines what the fund is supposed to do.

4. Risk—This section covers what types of events would cause the fund to lose value.

Information available on Vanguard's mutual funds include: historical total return performance data, bond fund yields and daily money market yields, portfolio manager profiles, and prospectus (34 different ones for 74 funds—every Vanguard fund available).

Fund Prices

Vanguard remains one of the industry leaders here as well, with an extensive returns section. Data available includes prices and average annual returns, daily NAVs, change in net asset from the previous day, year-to-date returns, and 1-, 5-, and 10-year average annual returns. A custom daily fund pricing function is also available, so that you may enter your own funds and get a quick update. Finally, money market and bond fund yields are update daily (by 6 p.m. or so).

Education

Here also Vanguard blows the competition away. This area is immense. A master's degree in investments and personal finance knowledge will be awarded if you make it through all these pages. Vanguard's Investor Education Center "has been an ardent proponent of increasing investor awareness and knowledge" and contains "an extraordinary amount of practical information about mutual fund investing—in a manner that can be directed by you."

It features three areas: University, which contains "courses" for novice investors; Library, which offers "in-depth materials about mutual fund investing and other general investment-related topics"; and, my favorite, the Laboratory, which has the latest technology experiments on display (previous features include a Java retirement calculator and the site Webmap).

If you want to learn more about the category a fund belongs to, click the category title at the upper-right corner of the profile.

Services

This area lists the myriad ways Vanguard can help you. Its subsections include several areas.

Catalog of Literature

I highly recommend touring this area. It contains useful information on software, literature, and services. Menu choices include software, literature library, newsstand, services directory, other mutual fund resources on the WWW, and tax planning WWW resources.

How to Contact

Phone, mail, and e-mail information is listed here.

Planning Tools

The Investment Personality area helps you find your risk tolerance. Unfortunately, though, you'll have to enter some info. But it's worth it.

Retirement Savings Calculator: to figure out the size of your nest egg.

Portfolio Planner: helps select which type of fund is right for you.

In addition to the four main sections, Vanguard's optional features worth exploring are the following:

- **About Vanguard/Mission Statement**—The only things in this area are the mission statement and an explanation of Vanguard's "unique corporate structure." If you're a believer in their philosophies, though, you'll enjoy reading through here.

- **What's News**—Announcements from Vanguard are included in this area.

- **Other Highlights**—Customized mutual fund reports, which allow investors to track their particular funds quickly, and the Investors education laboratory, which tests new features. Robert A. DiStefano, a senior information-technology VP, says, "Additional enhancements are planned. Our goal is to keep Vanguard in the forefront of mutual fund online services."

Vanguard Website Navigation Map

One of the most interesting features of Vanguard's site is the map to its entire site, as shown in Figure 10-6. Every Website should have one.

Vanguard's Table of Contents is immense, and it is another excellent feature that many other sites have adopted as well. The Table of Contents is shown in its entirety, just to impress upon you the sheer volume of information available on these Websites.

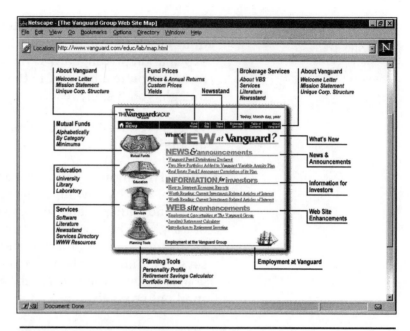

Figure 10-6. Vanguard's Website map is a helpful feature.

Table of Contents with Online University Courses

About Vanguard

Welcome Letter

Mission Statement

A Unique Corporate Structure

Vanguard Mutual Funds

Funds by Name

Funds by Category

Money Market Funds

Tax-Exempt Income Funds

State Tax-Exempt Income Funds

Fixed-Income Funds

Balanced Funds

Growth and Income Funds

Growth Funds

Aggressive Growth Funds

International Funds

Planning Tools

Your Investment Personality Profile

Retirement Savings Calculator

Portfolio Planner

Investor Education University

Learning Modules:

What Is a Mutual Fund ?

Building Your Portfolio

Selecting Specific Mutual Funds

Specialized Investments and
Approaches

Mutual Funds and Taxation

What Is a Mutual Fund?

Preview Quiz

Lesson 1: Mutual Fund Primer

Mutual Funds: Introduction

The Popularity and Advantages of
Mutual Funds

How to Invest in a Mutual Fund

How You Make Money in Funds

Taxes, Costs, and Risk of Ownership

**Lesson 2 What Is a Money Market
Fund?**

Describing Money Market Funds

Types of Money Market Funds

Money Market Funds: Advantages,
Risks, and Costs

Lesson 3: The ABC's of Bonds

Introducing Bonds

U.S. Government Bonds

Corporate Bonds

Municipal Bonds

A Glossary of Quality Ratings

The Risks and Rewards of Bonds

Bond Mutual Funds

**Lesson 4: An Introduction to Common
Stocks**

Defining Common Stocks

The Risks of Common Stocks

Recent Returns in Perspective

Investing in Common Stocks Through
Mutual Funds

A Word about Index Funds

**Lesson 5: The Risk/Return Trade-off
Investment Risk**

Market R\Risk

**Lesson 6: Defining Mutual Fund
Costs**

The Costs of Mutual Fund Investing

Determining Mutual Fund Costs

Comparing Mutual Fund Costs

Assessing the Impact of Costs

**Lesson 7: Understanding Mutual
Fund Documents**

Reading Mutual Fund Documents

Bogle on Retirement Investing

Vanguard Chairman Urges Rational Expectations for Future Stock Market Returns

Mutual Funds and Taxes

A Look at Tax-Adjusted Returns

The Benefits of Tax Deferral

Living Trusts: Pros and Cons

Tame the Tyranny of Taxes

Plain-Talk Series

Plain Talk about Realistic Expectations For Stock Market Returns

Plain Talk about Mutual Fund Costs

Plain Talk about Emerging Markets Investing

Plain Talk about Indexing

Retirement Planning

Getting the Most from Your Employer's Retirement Plan

FAQs about IRAs

FAQs about Retirement Plan Distributions

Bibliography

Glossary

Vanguard Catalog

Software

Retirement Planner Availability

How to Order

Literature Library

Vanguard Fund Express® Service

Manage Your Investments More Conveniently With Enhanced Vanguard Tele-Account®

Vanguard Plain Talk(sm) About Index Investing

The Vanguard Investment Planner

Facts on Funds®

Dollar-Cost Averaging

Vanguard Plain Talk(sm) About Investing In Emerging Markets

How to Be Your Own Investment Manager

The Company Behind Your Fund

Brokerage Services Exclusively For Vanguard Shareholders

Literature Library Order Form (Receive by U.S. Mail)

Vanguard Mutual Fund Prospectus Download

Vanguard Mutual Fund Prospectus Download Instructions

Services Directory

Service Terminology

Fund Minimum Initial Investments

Account Services

Account Services at a Glance

List of Available Account Services

Automatic Exchange Service

Vanguard Checkwriting

Vanguard Direct Deposit Service

Vanguard Dividend Express

Vanguard Fund Express

Vangard Wire Redemption

Compare Vanguard's Redemption Services

Vanguard Telephone Exchange

Vanguard Telephone Redemption

Investment Tracking

Your Newspaper's Mutual Fund Tables

Vanguard Account Statements

Fund Distributions

Individual Retirement Account Information

Other Mutual Fund Resources on the WWW

Employment

What's New

News and Announcements from Vanguard

Information for the Informed Investor

Web Site Enhancements

In The Vanguard, Winter 1996

Economist Considers Risks to Economy, Markets

Tax Matters: A Guide to YearEnd Tax Statements

Market Monitor: Fourth Quarter 1995 Market Review

Point: Counterpoint

To Make an IRA Contribution . . . or Not to Make an IRA Contribution.

Retirement Corner: The Pension Rollover Is A Smart Trick

Vanguard Fund Performance Profile (Daily Fund Prices)

Dazzled by Returns? Don't Forget Risk

News and Notes

In The Vanguard, Autumn 1995

Bull or Bear? Three Managers Offer Their Views

Investment Primer: Bond Yields Can Yield Some Confusion

Tax Planning: Yearend Tax Planning Considerations

Market Monitor: Third-Quarter Market Summary

Vanguard Fund Performance Profile (Daily Fund Prices)

Point: Counterpoint

Lump-Sum Investing: Higher Risk, Higher Potential

Dollar-Cost Averaging Simple and Sensible

Retirement Corner: Draw-Down Techniques During Retirement

Advanced Strategies: Vanguard Chairman Urges Rational Expectations for Future Stock Market

Returns

News and Notes

Your Opinion

Fund Prices

Contact Vanguard

Phone Service Directory

Vanguard Mail Services

E-mail Vanguard

For Vanguard Shareholders

General Information

Suggestions

Fund Information

For the New Investor

General Information

Suggestions

Fund Information

Most fund companies will have similar areas and features, though they'll have trouble matching the sheer volume of Vanguard's offerings. Please use the listing for reference when researching a specific issue.

Vanguard University

First, Vanguard University was available only on Vanguard Online, Vanguard's area on America Online, but now it has been transferred to Vanguard's Web site. This six-week course is the perfect introductory exposure to investing terms for novices. Following is a brief summary of the course topics:

- What is a mutual fund?

- Building your portfolio

- Selecting specific mutual funds

- Specialized investments and approaches

- Mutual funds and taxes

- Wrapping it all up

These topics give an excellent guided tour for those who need it, without any sales pressure. Look for future developments in the educational area at this site.

Vanguard Brokerage Services

If you do have individual stocks, the Vanguard discount brokerage arm offers competitive rates. Its commission schedule follows (visit the site for the latest amounts):

Principal multiplied by Factor Plus Base

$0 to $2,500	0.016 + $ 25
$2,501 to $5,000	0.0084 + $35
$5,001 to $15,000	0.004 + $60
$50,001 to $250,000	0.00125 + $ 100
$250,001 and Over	0.0011 + $ 125* *Negotiable

Vanguard Brokerage Services also offers FundAccess, its own mutual fund network (though with a fee). This network allows investors to purchase non-Vanguard funds at "a fixed $35 service fee that is assessed per order, not per share —regardless of share quantity. For purchases directly resulting from the sale of a FundAccess fund, a reduced fee of $30 is available on the purchase."

While investors could, of course, buy all of these other funds without the fee by going directly to the other fund company, this is a nice service for those who are primarily Vanguard investors. Fund groups available through this little-advertised program include: Twentieth Century/Benham, Brandywine, Cohen & Steers, Dreyfus, Fidelity, INVESCO, Janus, Mutual Series, Neuberger & Berman, Stein Roe, Strong, and Warburg Pincus.

Vanguard also has announced its own advisory service, which will perform a customized analysis for investors for a $500 fee. While most investors certainly won't require this level of service, there may be some complex cases that do. Expect some information about this service to be added to the site sometime in early 1997.

Finally, spokesperson John Woerth of Vanguard tells me that the company expects trading on the Web by early 1997 at the latest and that the company is moving away from its presence on America Online. As with Charles Schwab & Co.'s site, because it's on the cutting edge of the fund industry, even non-Vanguard investors should check in at **www.vanguard.com** occasionally just to see what its site is up to.

11

No-Load and Other Mutual Fund Sites

The following Web sites are mainly no-load funds', but I include a listing of almost every fund company that has a Web site. While some sites aren't as slick and extensive as the big boys', plenty of gems are available. I begin the chapter with Galt Technology's NETWorth, the fund super-site, then move to the T. Rowe Price site. Price's over $60 billion in assets makes it the fourth largest no-load fund group out there.

After that, I give brief synopses of the sites of Dreyfus, the third largest company, Twentieth Century/Benham, and Scudder, as well as the rest of the no-load companies with Web sites. For reasons expressed earlier, I concentrate on *families* of funds. Though I will mention "one-hit wonder" fund families, the better and bigger the company overall, the more space I devote to it.

I finish by listing several of the smaller no-load and other fund sites. If your fund company is anybody (on the Web), it should be listed in here (or in later chapters). Finally, full-service brokerage firms' sites, such as Prudential Securities and Merrill Lynch, are covered in the next chapter (following the discount brokerage sites).

Due to space and time constraints, I won't be able to mention every feature. So, needless to say, I will miss many places within these fund groups' sites. Don't let me stop you from exploring many of these sites, though, and check in often. These sites are being revamped, updated, and expanded all the time.

✳ Galt's NETWorth
networth.galt.com

Mega-Fund Site/Personal Finance Site
Pittsburgh, Pennsylvania

Content 📖📖📖   *Presentation* ☺☺☺   *Overall* 👍👍👍

Time You Should Spend There 🙂🙂
Don't Miss Feature-Fund Atlas
Strengt —Number of fund companies present 70+
Weakness—Too much "fee" data

Site Statistics: Over 1,000 pages
Number of Fund Sites: 73+

NAVs: Yes, Updated at 7 p.m.
News: No; Educational Materials: Yes

Sample Fund Families: Benham/Twentieth Century, Calvert, Dreyfus, Federated, Gabelli, IAI, Invesco, Janus, Montgomery, Neuberger&Berman, PBHG, Safeco, Scudder, and Stein Roe

Owned by Intuit, maker of Quicken personal financial software, this site contains over 70 different fund companies within its boundaries. While many of these fund groups are weaning themselves off NETWorth in order to launch their own proprietary sites, most continue to have a strong presence here. This is perhaps the biggest single mutual fund site on the Web, and with the added backing and linking-up of Quicken's Financial Network (qfn), this site promises to remain a top destination for fund investors.

Scott Cook, Chairman of Intuit, has stated, "We're big believers in the Internet." He says the Web in particular will "enable invention of new kinds of products and services that never existed before." The financial services community, in particular, should show innovation with the medium. He adds, "It's important to get good early."

Main Features

Mutual Fund Market Manager

Using data from Morningstar, the Chicago-based fund analysis company, the site offers fund profiles, screens of top performers, and more. Its *Fund Atlas* contains prospectuses and profiles of hundreds of funds, which may be accessed via a customized search engine. This allows users to locate potential funds by entering criteria, and it lists the top 25 funds in selected categories. Lists of the top 25 funds (among NETWorth's selected universe) ranked by year-to-date, 3-month, 1-year, 3-year, 5-year, and 10-year performance are also available.

Fund profiles from Morningstar are available as well, but the more detailed version will cost you. *Meet the Experts* often has knowledgeable fund industry guests, but you'll wind up hearing a lot of the standard market optimism for which fund managers are famous. Next, *Market Outlook* gives a decent recounting of recent market events, while *The Forum* involves more in-depth investment and financial planning issues.

The *Equities Center* includes several nice features. The Stock Quote Server is one of the best on the Web; NETWorth also has an Investor Relations Resource, access to Disclosure, and corporate earnings estimates (from I/B/E/S). The best feature here, though, is the Personal Portfolio, which allows users to construct their own fund and/or stock groupings and to receive updates on price and performance. It can track up to 50 items, but only one portfolio is allowed per user (for now).

NETWorth's *Financial Planner* contains one excellent educational resource, the Association of Individual Investors (discussed below). The rest of the section, though, is devoted to financial planning firms. Perspective Advisory Company, Fielder Financial Management, Ltd., Zurich Direct, and WebSaver are just a few of the financial firms with presences here. While these do have some helpful areas, I suggest readers avoid the sales pitches.

Finally, *The Insider* is devoted to links to other financial sites. It is a good place to check for new Web resources. The

Quicken Financial Network, which has extensive links to Galt's NETWorth site, will be covered in Chapter 13.

Commentary

Galt is a frequent destination of many online fund denizens, particularly now that Intuit's Quicken network has been so thoroughly integrated with NETWorth. (Intuit acquired Galt Technologies in 1995.) Its introductory screen is shown below in Figure 11-1.

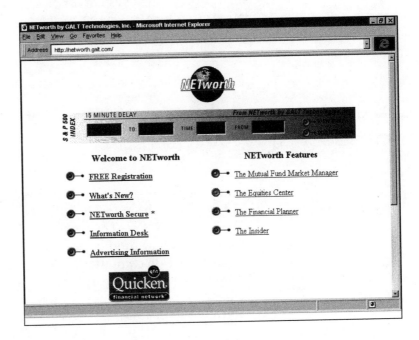

Figure 11-1. Galt Technology's NETWorth (Galt is owned by Quicken-maker Intuit)

Rob Frasca, president of GALT Technology, estimates that 4 to 6 percent of Internet users of the Galt site who request information will invest money with a fund company. While this may seem small to some, it represents enormous potential for fund companies. As traffic on the World Wide Web grows, more and more asset-gathering will take place via this channel.

Galt has been involved heavily with the fund companies for some time now, and as functions linking banking, investing, and other personal finance tasks become integrated, expect Galt and Quicken to be there. So, visit every once in a while to see what's brewing. This site is a huge all-around source of information. It also allows for information "shopping" using CyberCash, a system for encrypting credit card information. (I return to the subject of online transactions in Chapters 15 and 16.)

AAII (American Association of Individual Investors) www.aaii.org

Among the many organizations that have set up shop on GALT, one you should visit is the American Association of Individual Investors. This organization lists an extensive number of mutual fund basics topics, and it has one of the best overviews on computerized investing around at its site. Though it's a little lengthy and somewhat dated, it is an excellent source for reviews on investment software (it may be found at www.ai.org/ci/computer.html).

AAII's home page greeting says that the organization "provides educational material to help individuals become better managers of their money." It isn't affiliated with any financial organizations and doesn't recommend specific investments, making it a truly objective source of information. AAII says that its "Web pages can help everyone— from novices learning the basics to more advanced investors involved in fundamental stock analysis and screening."

One of its strengths is the computerized investing area. Its annual *Individual Investor's Guide to Computerized Investing* lists almost every software program for investing available. Plus, AAII has a computer-investor newsletter, *Computerized Investing*. Finally, AAII's site includes an excellent primer on using your computer for investing at its site, so please take a look.

As we'll see, there are plenty of other independent organizations that offer educational materials. We'll investigate many of these in the following sections.

☀ T. Rowe Price Associates, Inc.
www.troweprice.com

No-Load Fund Family
800/638-5660 Baltimore, Maryland

Content 📖📖📖 *Presentation* ☺☺☺☺ *Overall* 👍👍👍👍

Time You Should Spend There ⏱⏱
Don't Miss Feature-Investment Strategies
Strength—Educational information
Weakness—Depth

Site Statistics: Several hundred pages of info

Fund Family Statistics: Assets—$80+ billion; Funds—67; Other—Known for international and growth funds

NAVs: Yes, updated at 7 p.m.
News: Yes
Educational Materials: Yes

Fund Performance Numbers:1-yr; 3-yr; 5-yr; nice format

The site is divided into three main areas: What's News, which contains some decent but usually dated weekly commentary, access to DBC's daily updates and quotes; Mutual Fund Info (below); and Retirement Planning, which has a host of interactive but simple planning tools. The following data may be found under Mutual Fund Info:

The Four "P's":
Prices, Performance, Prospectus, and Profiles

Like most other fund sites, Price's includes an NAV feature listing daily prices and changes (available in Quicken download format) grouped by fund type. Fund performance includes YTD, 1-yr, 3-yr, and 5-yr, plus 10-yr or since inception, whichever is longer, but the data is only as of the end of the latest month. (A customized "watch list" is also available.)

T. Rowe's fund profiles are well done, including hard-to-find statistics such as fund sector weightings, but they could use more up-to-date information. And, prospectuses may be downloaded (using the ubiquitous Adobe Acrobat reader) or sent via regular mail.

Library

This library contains a very readable selection of general information, investment strategies (which I recommend), and a host of articles on types of investment instruments.

On-Line Access

Price shareholders may access 401(k) account information to check balances, investment allocations, and prices, and they may also make trades (via AOL). Approximately 200,000 of 550,000 qualified participants are potential users of the system, though initially only 10 to 20 percent are expected to utilize it. The Home Page for T. Rowe Price is pictured in Figure 11-2.

Institutional Area

This recently added section caters to T. Rowe Price's 401(k), 403(b), and 457 retirement plan participants. (These numbers represent the section of the tax code from whence their exemptions from immediate taxation spring.) One feature this section shares with Price's main site is a *watch list* of funds chosen by the user. Retirement investors are able to access a profiling tool, which allows users to detail their risk tolerance, time frame, and other factors. The content displayed all flows from this profile. "Customization, not general-interest material, encourages return trips to a site," says T. Rowe Price's Tom Mayer, a vice president of retirement

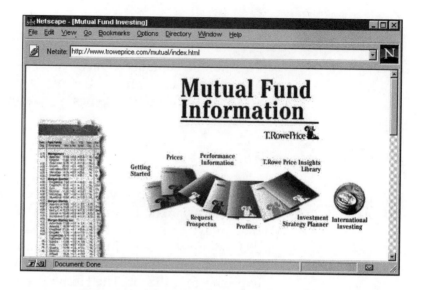

Figure 11-2. The mutual fund section of T. Rowe Price's site rates high for education and international fund information.

services. Finally, several useful retirement planning tools and articles are also available.

Commentary

This Baltimore, Maryland, fund company is one of the largest no-load companies. T. Rowe Price's international funds, in particular, have gained a huge following. While not as extensive as the big 2's (Fidelity and Vanguard) sites, it nonetheless is a nice example of what a fund company's site should provide. Price's site has: fund profiles, daily prices, performance information and yields on any Price fund; prospectus download, an introduction to fund investing, library, and more.

Not only are T. Rowe Price's international funds excellent, but the international section of its Website is also outstanding.

The fundamentals of international markets and weekly over-seas updates may be found here.

Trading is available on AOL only, though T. Rowe Price hopes to have this function added to its Web site in the near future. On America Online, investors can download prospectuses, check prices, and receive performance information.

Other No-Load Fund Groups

✳ Dreyfus Funds/Mellon Bank
www.dreyfus.com

No-Load Fund Family
800/221-1793 x8255 Pittsburgh, Pennsylvania

Content 📖📖 *Presentation* ☺ *Overall* ♨

Time You Should Spend There ☺
Don't Miss Feature-Automatic Investing Model

Fund Family Statistics: Assets—$80+ billion; Funds—100; Other—Good bond, money funds

Strength—At least they have a site
Weakness—Design

NAVs: No News: No (some market commentary)
Educational Materials: Yes

As you would expect from such a conservative company, Dreyfus's Website is pretty standard (and pretty boring). This company, known for its bond and money market funds, has been busy with its assimilation into new parent Mellon Bank. So, it is understandably behind in the competition on the Web. While this isn't quite what you'd expect from one of the largest fund companies, there will probably be additions and a revamp in the future.

It does have a couple of nice features, though, like weekly commentary from oft-quoted economist Richard Hoey. The Strategies sections merely list which Dreyfus funds are appropriate for what types of investing. The site is skimpy, but if you're a Dreyfus investor, you probably aren't concerned with surfing the Web, anyway. You're probably just sitting back collecting those fat bond or money market dividend checks.

✳ Scudder, Stevens, & Clark
funds.scudder.com

No-Load Fund Family
800/225-2470 Boston, Massachusetts

Content 📖📖 *Presentation* ☺☺☺☺ *Overall* 👍👍👍

Time You Should Spend There 🕐🕐
Don't Miss Feature -Performance Data
Strength—International fund info
Weakness—Up-to-date fund info

Site Statistics: Over 500 pages;
Online account access and trading in late 1996

Fund Family Statistics: Assets—$35+ billion; Funds—39; Other—On Prodigy in 1988

NAVs: Yes, updated at 7 p.m.
News: Yes; Educational Materials: Yes

Fund Performance Numbers:1-yr; 3-yr; 5-yr; nice format; Daily performance data by Lipper

Scudder, like T. Rowe Price, is also strong internationally, and it has a pretty standard Website. It, too, has the four "P's"—prices, performance, profiles (fund), and prospectuses. Its major areas include: About Scudder, Global Investing, Funds, Planning (which is somewhat sparse), and News (which also is pretty much press releases).

Another option, the site's Personal Page, allows users to enter their preferences for funds and performance information, so when you check in you get a customized brief (an e-mail option probably isn't far off). But this is mainly just a way to get you to enter some of your statistics. The bulk of the useful stuff is found in the Funds section.

In addition to the retail area, there is a section for 401(k) investors and one for RIAs (registered investment advisors). These contain some interesting exercises and readings, but not much else. Overall, the site is just so-so, attractive only to Scudder investors. While the fund prospectuses do have an extensive amount of textual information, they're light on data such as fund holdings.

However, this could well change in the coming months because Scudder just now appears to be making a serious investment into technology and marketing. The Scudder family as a whole is excellent; I wouldn't hesitate to recommend it. It bills itself as a *pure* no-load fund family, which means no 12b-1 fees, either.

✳ Twentieth Century/Benham Funds www.twentieth-century.com

NETWorth address: networth.galt.com/www/home/mutual/
twntyth/twntyth.htm

No-Load Fund Family
800/345-2021 Kansas City, Missouri

Content 📖📖📖 *Presentation* ☺☺☺☺☺ *Overall* 💧💧💧💧

Time You Should Spend There ⏱⏱⏱
Don't Miss Feature—"Tree Map"
Strength—Design, Stock Fund Info
Weakness—Material

Site Statistics: Over 1,000 pages; Also site on AOL

*Fund Family Statistics: Assets—$50+ billion; Funds—50+;
Other—Known for growth funds*

NAVs: Yes, Updated at 7 p.m. News: Yes
Educational Materials: Yes

Fund Performance Numbers: 1-yr; 3-yr; 5-yr; nice format

Main Features

Twentieth Century plans offering account access via the Internet in the fourth quarter of 1996. This site's features include:

The "Menu Tree"

This is one of the most useful features of any site. It consists of a map in the upper-right corner of the screen, which grows as users visit different pages. This pull-down menu highlights the section you're currently in and offers an easy means of returning to any previously visited sections. In addition, the overall navigational planning that went into Twentieth Century's site makes it quite simple to use. The standard navigational buttons are plentiful and visible.

Fund Performance and Profiles

Daily pricing of NAVs (updated by 7 p.m.) and historical return data may be found here. The individual fund profiles for each Twentieth Century fund may be accessed here; these give in-depth info, including objectives, investment strategies, minimums, and expenses. Twentieth Century goes above and beyond its competitors in giving access to its funds' top holdings, top sectors, and more. While the performance numbers are slightly dated, overall this site ranks in the top 5 percent.

Portfolio Tracker

This feature enables you to enter up to 10 demo portfolios (with up to 30 funds or stocks in each), making checking prices a breeze.

Site Search

This is a button that allows users to enter keywords or phrases, and searches the site for references. A glossary of investment terms is also included for good measure.

About/News/Contacting

As with most, Twentieth Century/Benham's other options provide users with "information about [the] company, press releases, seminars and how to contact."

✳ Janus Funds www.janusfunds.com

No-Load Fund Family
800/525-8983 Denver, Colorado

Content 📖 *Presentation* ☺☺ *Overall* 👍👍

Don't bother with this one. Though Janus has had a reputation for go-go growth funds, many of which invest in technology, it's clear that they are not on the cutting edge as far as Web sites go.

Janus investors, however, may want to bookmark this URL to check performance information occasionally, while others who are considering a Janus fund can find Fund Profiles. The information is a little sparse, though.

✳ Strong Funds, Inc. www.strong-funds.com

No-Load Fund Family
800/368-1030 Milwaukee, Wisconsin

Content 📖 *Presentation* ☺☺☺☺ *Overall* 👍👍👍

Strong's offerings include the following sections: News, Retirement Investing, Learning Center, About Strong, Managing Your Portfolio, and Fund Performance. In addition, *Real Audio* sound features, like portfolio manager interviews, are available on the site. (Strong was the first fund family with Real Audio on its site.) All in all, this Website looks very nice and is well done, but it doesn't offer non-Strong investors much in the way of general investment information. Within the retirement investing area, though, there is an excellent example of five "asset allocation models" that investors may want to check out.

Among Strong's 30 funds (including the Schaefer Value fund, which Strong purchased in the past year), Strong's money market funds in particular stand out. Strong Heritage, which is waiving its management fees, is among the top money funds in the country, while Strong Money Market has been one of the highest yielding over the past several years.

✳ Invesco Funds Group
www.invesco.com

No-Load Fund Family
800/525-8085 Kansas City, Missouri

Content 📖📖 *Presentation* ☺☺☺☺ *Overall* 🌢🌢🌢

While primarily geared toward institutional investors, which make up the bulk of its clientele, the INVESCO site is sleek and well done. However, unless you're a shareholder, you're better off sticking with the sites geared primarily to individual investors. Figure 11-3 shows this page.

The Individual Investors section is where to find the most useful data. Under Beginning Investors there is a useful "build your own portfolio" exercise, while the Advanced Investors section contains comments from portfolio managers, other investment links, and access to portfolio profiles. These are rather skimpy, though.

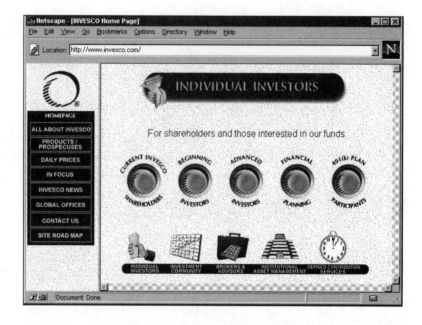

Figure 11-3. Invesco's site is geared for both institutional and retail customers.

✳Stein Roe Funds   networth.galt.com/ www/home/mutual/steinroe/

✳ Liberty Financial Companies (parent) www.lib.com

No-Load Fund Family
800/338-2550 Boston, Massachusetts

Content 📖📖📖 *Presentation* ☺☺☺ *Overall* 👍👍👍

The Stein Roe no-load family of mutual funds may be found here. Their Stein Roe Young Investor fund is featured prominently at both sites, as is Liberty's insurance expertise. The Colonial Mutual funds may be found at Liberty's site. Finally, a list of financial links is provided.

The setup is pretty standard: Mutual Fund Directory, What's Hot, Investor Tools, Market Insights, Mutual Fund, Glossary, Stein Roe Information. Directory lists their information on their funds and investing; What's Hot is recent releases; Investor Tools and Market Insights are both rather sparse; the *Glossary* is good.

The best feature so far is the Market Insights area, which has monthly market and economic commentary. The commmentaries are well-written and informative, but they aren't enough to cause me to advise non-Stein Roe investors to visit the site. All around, it is a decent showing for a smaller fund company.

Smaller No-Load Sites In Brief

✳ Montgomery Funds
networth.galt.com/www/home/mutual/montgomery

No-Load Fund Family
800/572-3863 San Francisco, California

Content 📖📖 *Presentation* ☺☺ *Overall* 👍👍

The Montgomery Group, located on Galt's NETWorth, is the sponsor of this site's Meet the Experts feature. The Montgomery area itself, however, doesn't have much to offer other than prospectus downloads and minimal fund performance data. Parent Montgomery Securities also has a site at www.montgomery.com.

✳ IAI Mutual Funds
networth.galt.com/IAIwww/home/mutual/iai/

No-Load Fund Family
800/945-3863 Minneapolis, Minnesota

Content 📖 *Presentation* ☺ *Overall* 👍

This site is the bare minimum for a large, diversified fund company like IAI. However, at least it's quick and easy to navigate. The fund descriptions themselves do give you a good idea of which fund would be the right one for a certain situation. Finally, though there's little to bring you here, the company does have decent-performing funds. IAI has 14 funds and over $15 billion under management.

✳ Robertson Stephens www.rsim.com

No-Load Fund Family
800/766-3863 San Francisco, California

Content 📖📖📖 *Presentation* ☺☺☺ *Overall* ♨♨♨

Robertson Stephens & Co., of San Francisco, is known for its high-octane Value+Growth fund, as well as its Contrarian and Information Age funds. Given its expertise in the technology area (its investment banking specialty is here), you'd expect an impressive Web site. Well, it delivers, partially. The site has some interesting features, such as Real Audio manager commentary and customized portfolio features, but the information on each fund is rather limited.

The In the News feature is original—it contains reprints of recent articles from popular media outlets about Robertson Stephens' funds. Within the fund information area, the portfolio summary option gives investors an excellent look at the sectors and stocks in which each fund invests. Finally, prospectuses may be viewed online, and daily NAVs are posted.

✳ Calvert www.calvertgroup.com

Fund Family
800/368-2748 Bethesda, Maryland

Content 📖📖📖 *Presentation* ☺☺☺☺ *Overall* ♨♨♨♨

Though most of socially-responsible Calvert Group's customers purchase their funds through brokers, no-load customers can find some decent things at this site, too. The site started in earnest in December 1995, and it has been averaging approximately 3,000 to 4,000 visitors a month. In January 1996, Calvert was the first fund family to offer online account access.

Two areas of particular interest are its Guide to Mutual Funds and Socially Responsible options. The former has a very readable overview of funds and investing, while the latter explains the basics and Calvert's role in this field. Even though it is mainly a marketing pitch, investors who are interested in learning more about this area should check the Calvert site out.

✳ Gabelli Funds, Inc. www.gabelli.com

No-Load Fund Family
800/422-3554 New York, New York

Content 📖📖 *Presentation* ☺☺ *Overall* 💧💧

The Gabelli funds were some of the first to offer account access online, but the site overall is a little sparse. The site does contain several worthwhile articles within its Investor Education Center, including features on investing for retirement, fund taxation, variable annuities, and dollar-cost averaging.

Gabelli, which has profiles available online for download, plans to add trading to its site by the end of 1996. Finally, if you're looking for the Interactive Couch Potato Fund, which specializes in "multimedia" technology companies, this is the place.

✳ GIT Funds, Inc. www.gitfunds.com

No-Load Fund Family
800/336-3063 Arlington, Virginia

Content 📖📖 *Presentation* ☺☺ *Overall* 👆👆

I've included the GIT funds because they were the first group to actually list daily portfolio holdings (and changes) on their site. This demonstrated such openness and gumption among the fund industry that I had to single GIT out for praise. I hope other groups will eventually follow its lead.

The site is decent, with some articles, the ability to download prospectuses, and performance information. However, sometimes tit has been a couple of days behind with updates.

✳ SAFECO Mutual Funds
networth.galt.com/www/home/
mutual/safeco

No-Load Fund Family
800/426-6730 Seattle, Washington

Content 📖📖 *Presentation* ☺☺☺ *Overall* 👆👆

SAFECO is a large insurance company in the Pacific Northwest that owns a family of 17 no-load mutual funds. Its Web site is somewhat sparse, but it does have a nice basic financial planning overview. Other information includes fund profiles (via NETWorth's Fund Atlas), ordering information, and a section for institutional services.

Other Financial Company Fund Group Sites

Many other companies offer mutual funds, but I've only listed one example here. More are included with the bank-owned fund groups among the Banking section of Chapter 13, while brokerages with fund groups are listed at the end of the Chapter 12, Discount Brokers.

Although some of these sights do have excellent educational and market data features, I suggest that investors avoid all other fund groups except the pure no-loads. Banks and full-service brokers, though many have "no-load" funds, tend to have much higher expenses than the no-load families themselves.

✳ Massachusetts Financial Services www.mfs.com

Content 📖📖 *Presentation* ☺☺☺☺ *Overall* 👍👍👍

Though the MFS funds are mainly sold through advisors and brokers, I've listed its home page due to its massive total asset size. It has an extensive educational section on working with a financial advisor for those of you who do need help, and it also has some market data and commentary.

12

Discount Brokers

The earliest and most aggressive players among financial companies moving onto the Web are the discount brokers, especially the "deep-discount" brokers, or those that charge extremely low flat fees and offer little in the way of services. These firms, which charge as little as $10 per trade, see the Internet as a match made in heaven. Due to the extremely low costs involved in trading—customer service is now done electronically, there are no branches, and mailing costs are nil—these companies are now able to compete with the larger, more service-oriented firms. Their nimbleness allowed them to seize a significant piece of the new online trading market.

These companies appeared early in 1995, and initially they caused quite a scare among the brokerage community, especially among the larger brokerage houses. However, the big discount brokers—Schwab, Jack White, and others—didn't sit still. They leapt onto the Internet, slashing their commissions to protect their turf. While it remains to be seen just how much of the market the deep-discount Internet brokers will hold onto, many of these companies are here to stay.

Phoebe Simpson, an analyst at Internet consulting firm Jupiter Communications, summarizes the confict: "Online brokerage has come to the forefront in recent months as perhaps the perfect mix of the Internet and financial services. At the same time, it is an excellent example of the threat that online financial services pose to cannibalize traditional systems. Electronic trading may push the brokers out of brokerage."

She says that the main reason these discounters are so attractive is this: "Many consumer are already wired and use their PCs for financial news and information. They are looking for more applications that will save them money." Though, as I warn later in this chapter, there are many hidden fees and trade-offs involved in going with the cheaper companies, for self-directed investors the best among them represent excellent alternatives.

While many of the mutual fund companies we've reviewed are still reluctant to add full fund trading to their sites, the discount brokers have been trading funds for some time now. Companies like Quick & Reilly and Jack White & Co. have been allowing trading via proprietary software bulletin boards and automated telephone services for over a decade now. They've pioneered the idea of online trading, and they continue to be at the forefront as the Internet takes over as the trading vehicle of choice.

Most of the following companies offer funds as well as stocks and other securities, though most charge a small commission or transaction fee to buy and sell. Only Schwab and a few others offer their own funds; most allow access to other families' funds as a service for their investors. Along with each site, I list the types and number of funds available for trading on each "marketplace," plus the commissions for trading funds.

Initially, fund trading was offered as a convenience for existing shareholders. It should soon become a profit center in its own right, especially if some of the large fund groups take much longer to offer full trading. With the number of online accounts approaching 1 million, these customers will only grow in importance. (There are approximately 60 million brokerage accounts total.)

I've already mentioned the threat that this new breed of discounters poses to both the traditional discount brokers and especially to the full-service brokers, but I wanted to briefly return to this theme. As one expert said, "If you can get information and trading over the Internet, why do you need a broker?" Another says, "The Internet is a big threat to the current system. I think the full-service firms are worried about it."

While the full-service brokers have managed to survive the discount broker and 800-number revolution, their clientele is literally dying off. Younger investors have shown a preference for self-directed trading and the Internet, so don't be surprised if even the Smith Barney's and Prudential's of the world begin to offer cut-rate trading options via the World Wide Web. (Already, they are offering no-load funds.)

In this chapter, I briefly talk about the largest of the deep discount brokers. I begin with the PAWWS Financial Network, which contains Jack White & Co., sponsor of the largest "mutual fund network," and several other discount brokers within its pages. I also review Internet pioneers Lombard Securities and E*Trade, then mention several of the smaller players in the discount area. Finally, I close with a listing of full-service and other firms that have Web sites. While I advise against investing with these high-cost providers, their sites do have a few interesting and useful areas which we'll visit.

✳ PAWWS Financial Network www.pawws.com

Content 📖📖📖 *Presentation* ☺☺☺ *Overall* ♠♠♠

Like many other sites, PAWWS (which stands for Portfolio Accounting World-Wide Service) attempts to be a "one-stop shopping" financial site, which provides portfolio accounting, quotes, and research in addition to online brokerage services. More brokerages and content providers are expected to join the site, which is receiving hundreds of thousands of hits a day.

This unit of Security APL (Chicago), which offers accounting systems to money managers and is a subsidiary of CheckFree Corp., houses several large discount brokers. Particular attention will be paid to Jack White & Co., the largest of these discounters and a major player in the "no-transaction-fee" mutual fund network business.

In addition to Jack White, the site contains areas for Howe Barnes' *The Net Investor* and The Sherwood Group's *National*

Discount Broker (NDB). These three discount broker subdivisions offer an attractive combination, due to their different levels of service and price. The PAWWS site also contains plenty of market data, including IPO and fundamental research data and offers extensive portfolio accounting options.

Rick Griffin, a senior vice president at Howe Barnes, sums up investing on the Internet, "You have a lot more freedom, and you don't run into ads when you sign on. The Internet has more potential than interactive TV. It is here, it is economical, provides easy access, and most people have the equipment to handle it. I think the Internet will prove as significant to society as the telephone."

✳ Jack White & Co.'s PATH On-Line pawws.com/jwc

Content 📖📖📖 *Presentation* ☺☺☺ *Overall* ♨♨♨♨

Commissions: $33 + 3 cents/share (< 2,000 shares); $33 + 2 cents/sh (>=2,000 shares).

Fund Trading? Y
Number of Funds 800 No-Fee 4,200 Total.

Fund fees Up to $5,000—$27; $5,001-$25,000—$35; $25,001 and above—$50.

Jack White & Co. was the first firm to offer fund trading on the Internet, after surveys had indicated that over 64 percent of its investors used PCs. This firm was also the first to offer mutual funds with no transaction fees (1984) and the first to offer a fund "network" (1992). Jack White accounts on the Internet have minimums of $5,000 (versus $500 for a normal account) to attract more advanced investors. Its site on the PAWWS network is shown in Figure 12-1.

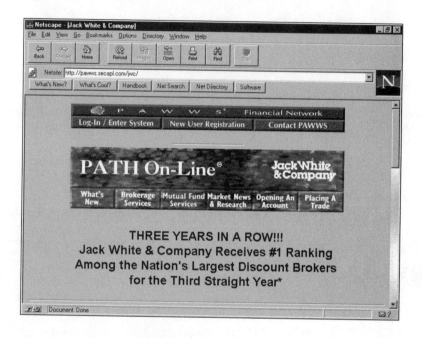

Figure 12-1. Jack White's giving Schwab a run for its money in fund networks.

Another option for Jack White users is its ComputerPATH software ($30). This proprietary system lets users place trades and also check accounts. While I personally prefer Schwab due to its slightly higher level of service and proprietary index funds, White does have an advantage as far as costs go. For active traders, it is an excellent place to consolidate individual stocks, funds, and other securities.

✳ National Discount Brokers
pawws.com/ndb

Content 📖📖 *Presentation* ☺☺ *Overall* 👍👍

Brokerage Commissions: $20 OTC stocks; $25 other (plus $3 and 1 cent per share > 5k).

Fund Trading Yes
Number of Funds almost 300 no-load, no-fee
Fund fees $34-$85

With commissions of $20 a trade, it's not hard to see why companies like National Discount Brokers have begun to take market share from the bigger discount and full-service firms. Their FundVest program offers almost 300 no-fee funds. As with other brokers with rock-bottom commissions, watch out for extra fees here.

✳ Net Investor (Howe Barnes
Investments) pawws.com/tni

Content 📖 *Presentation* ☺ *Overall* 👍

Commissions $29 plus 2.5 cents/share on first 3,000 shares; 1.5 cents per share thereafter.

Fund Trading? Yes (w/fees);
Fund fees $35 (<$15k); $45 ($15k<$100k); $60 ($100k).

This site has the claim to being the "first fully integrated investment and portfolio management system on the Internet." It went online in January 1995, and it continues to offer deep discounts on brokerage trades. Its parent, Howe Barnes Investments, is a regional brokerage in Chicago.

The Net Investor provides online portfolio reporting, historical and intra-day price graphs, company research, Morningstar mutual fund reports, real-time quotes (based on number of trades), checking, VISA, and earnings forecasts. It claims that its "advanced system automatically works to price improve qualified NASDAQ orders, potentially saving you hundreds of dollars."

✳ Lombard Securities
www.lombard.com

Content 📖📖📖 *Presentation* ☺☺☺☺ *Overall* 💧💧💧💧

Commissions: $34 (1-1,700 shares), 2 cents/share (over 1,700 shares); $34 for OTC.

Fund Trading? Planned but not available yet.
800/LOMBARD

Lombard was the first of the "deep-discounters" to offer trading through the Internet, in late March 1995. This subsidiary of Thomas F. White & Co. of San Francisco (Lombard's home) was rated number one among discount brokers in *Barron's* first ranking of these firms. Over 20 percent of the company's trading now comes from online sources; this number is expected to top 50 percent by early 1998.

The company, like many of the other upstarts, has been upgrading its computer systems, so users shouldn't have to worry about heavy-use periods. But, of course, as with all online trading, you're dependent on many technical factors—phone lines, power, and computer hardware and software. This is why it's usually worth it to pay the little extra commission for a larger company in order to get a degree of extra service.

✳ E*Trade www.etrade.com

Content 📖 *Presentation* ☺☺☺ *Overall* 👍👍

Fund Trading? No
Brokerage Commissions: $14.95 listed securities, $19.95 OTC

"All roads lead to the Internet," says E*Trade's chairman and founder William Porter. This Palo Alto, California, company, one of the earliest with live trading on the Web, has gained business due to its low, low commissions. For trades of up to 5,000 shares on the NYSE or AMEX (New York or American exchanges), the cost is $14.95, while it's $19.95 for NASDAQ (over-the-counter) stocks. Account minimums are only $1,000; $2,000 for margin accounts.

Investment information is available at the site to both customers and non-customers alike. Links and updates from

CNNfn, Dead Man's Island (an individual stock-picking site), EDGAR, Hoover's, Stockmaster, and WSJ-IA may be found here. (Figure 12-2 depicts E*Trades site.)

Jupiter Communications Phoebe Simpson adds, "But despite E*Trade's skyrocket success, the company has been plagued by service complaints, bringing into question the company's ability to handle increasing volume. Online bulletin board posting were legion following one market downturn when lines became jammed."

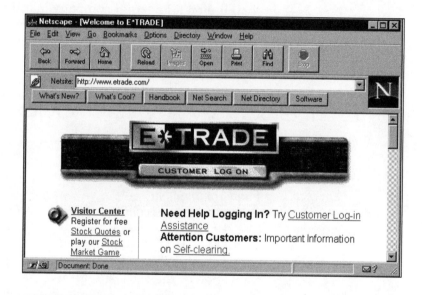

Figure 12-2. Deep, deep discount brokers like E*Trade appeared early on the Net.

While the company has continued to increase capacity, its problems illustrate one reason why customers would want to pay the extra amount to invest with a Schwab or other giant that they know will make good on any problems or system failures.

Watch Out for Fees!

Many of the so-called "deep discounters" survive on fees. For example, here is a recent schedule of fees from E*Trade. The commissions are low, but beware the total cost. Be sure to consider any restrictions before jumping with the low-cost provider.

1. Account Transfers Out — $20.00
2. Certificate Transfer Out (in account holder name) — $5.00
3. Certificate Transfer Out (in name other than that of account holder) — $10.00
4. Overnight Mail (upon request) — $15.00
5. Returned Customer Checks — $25.00
6. Wired Funds Out — $20.00
7. Stop Payment Request On E*Trade Check — $15.00
8. "Restricted" Securities (such as those subject to Rule 144) — $75.00
9. Fed Call Extensions — $10.00
10. Voluntary Reorganizations — $20.00
11. Account research requests will be charged $5 for the first statement and $2.50 for each statement thereafter.
12. Real-time quote fees:
    Non-Professional Subscriber: $30/month
    Professional Subscriber: $191.10/month
    Connect Time ...

See E*-Trades site for current fees.

E*Trade also has plans to enter the investment banking and venture capital business on the Web (which I discuss further in Chapter 15, "Buying and Selling Online"). This is certainly an attractive option for investors who are very concerned about price.

✳ Quick & Reilly
www.quick&reilly.com

Content 📖📖📖 *Presentation* ☺☺☺ *Overall* 👍👍👍

Brokerage Commissions: $37.50
Online trading through QuickWay Plus software only.

This was one of the original "deeper" discount brokers. While it hasn't yet established Web trading, it does give investors the option to order the QuickWay Plus software (below) for making trades. Overall, Q&R does an excellent job, but it is more expensive than some of the others (and doesn't have the features of Schwab).

QuickWay Plus Software

A very nice package all around, this free software can make trades, perform portfolio management functions, and call up research reports through the Reuters Money Network (there is a charge for this service). Trading through this system gives users a 10 percent discount. Its Easy Trade touch-tone telephone program gives 10 percent discounts also.

✳ OLDE Discount Brokers
www.oldenet.com

Content 📖 *Presentation* ☺ *Overall* 👍

There is no trading as of yet on the OLDE site, but I've included it because it is one of the most well-known discount brokerages. OLDE (800/USA-OLDE) is known for its money market fund, which is consistently among the top-yielding in the country. (However, this is often due to the fund waiving fees on its expenses, so investors will want to watch the yield carefully in case fees are reinstated.)

Other Discount Brokerage Companies

✳ PC Financial Network www.pcfn.com

Content 📖📖📖📖 *Presentation* ☺☺☺☺ *Overall* 🔥🔥🔥

Brokerage Commissions: $40 (base)
800/TALK-PCF

This company, a subsidiary of the Pershing division of Donaldson, Lufkin & Jenrette (DLJ) Securities Corp., bills itself as "America's Largest Online Discount Broker." PCFN has been on the Prodigy service for years now; its commissions, however, are slightly higher than competitors'. The usual service options, including trading, account data and research, are available, and there is an extra commission savings for "frequent traders."

Its parent, DLJ, which is the largest clearing firm (handling 10 percent of trade accounting) on the New York Stock Exchange, also runs Net Exchange, a customized area with home pages for other broker/dealers providing account information and trading for a group of smaller brokerages.

✳ Accutrade www.accutrade.com

Content 📖📖📖 *Presentation* ☺☺ *Overall* 👍👍

Fund Trading? Yes
Number of Funds 5,000+ Total
Fund fees $27 (no-loads)
Brokerage Commissions: $28 + 2 cents a share.
800/494-8939

Accutrade has a nice setup and very reasonable fees, plus they give investors extensive access to fund trading. Once all fees are taken into account, this is one of the lowest-cost providers. Their Website is also attractive and easy to navigate.

✳ K. Aufhauser's WealthWeb www.aufhauser.com

Content 📖📖📖 *Presentation* ☺☺☺ *Overall* 👍👍👍

Fund fees$0-$4,999—$34; $5,000-$9,999—$40; $10,000 or more—$50
800/870-9671

Brokerage Commissions: 1 - 399 shares $24.99; 400 - 1700 $34.00; 1700+ 2 cents/ share
(10 percent discount on all equity orders placed over automated systems.)

This New York-based company offered the first Internet stock trades at the end of 1994, and it has accepted fund trades since 1995. President Keith Aufhauser commented about the pleasing demographics of Web investors. "We're looking for the intelligent investor, so we're happy to take the upper crust," he says. All in all, the Aufhauser site is pretty good, and the commissions are quite reasonable.

✳ Ceres Securities, Inc. www.ceres.com

Content 📖📖📖 *Presentation* ☺☺☺ *Overall* 👍👍👍

800-669-3900
Brokerage Commissions: $18

There's been online trading at this subsidiary of Omaha-based TransTerra Co. since May 1996, when Ceres's flat rate of $18 a trade began causing a stir among online investors. The site includes quotes, trades and account balances, and commentary from tax guru and business columnist Andrew Tobias. Over 20 percent of its trades now take place online. President Mary Fay says, "Our customers like to do things their own way, manage and execute their own investments. Technological advances allow us to make this possible at great cost savings, which are passed along to the people who trade with us."

✳ E*Broker www.ebroker.com

Content 📖 *Presentation* ☺☺ *Overall* 👍👍

This company charges only $12 a trade, making it the absolute cheapest available. It is also known as All-American Brokers, and it is owned (as are the two preceding companies, Accutrade and Aufhauser, plus another online firm, Ceres Securities) by TransTerra of Omaha, Nebraska.

While it may be an appropriate choice for some thrifty investors, most will probably want to go with a larger company ... just in case.

✳ A. G. Edwards www.agedwards.com

Content 📖📖📖📖 *Presentation* ☺☺☺☺ *Overall* 👍👍👍👍

This St. Louis brokerage has a very nice site. As expected, the mid-sized, regional brokerages have more incentive to bring in business through their sites because their sales force is smaller than the large brokerages. This site is updated weekly and contains news, market and economic commentary, office locations, and some financial planning tools.

The following chart compares the features of the sites discussed so far in Chapter 12.

Online Trading on the Web

Table 12-1 Comparing the Discount Brokerages

Service/800#	Parent Company	URL/other	Minimum Commission	Comments
Accutrade 800/494-8939	TransTerra Omaha, NE	`www.accutrade.com` Touchtone; PDA	$28 plus $0.02/sh	Users can set up automatic trades.
Ceres Securities 800/669-3900	TransTerra	`www.ceres.com`	$18	No min., but $20 charge for < $1000.
eBroker 800/553-9513	All-American (TransTerra)	`www.ebroker`	$12	same as Ceres.
e.Schwab 800/540-0667	Charles Schwab SF, CA	`www.schwab.com` Direct dial	$39 (StreetSmart trades are higher)	10% discount.
E*Trade n/a	Trade*Plus Palo Alto, CA	`www.etrade.com` AOL, Compuserve	$15	Lowest fees; $30/mo for real time quotes.
Fidelity Brokerage 800/544-0246	Fidelity Investment Boston, MA	`swww.fid-inv.com` Fidelity Online Express	contact for rates (FOX) software	Services galore.
Lombard 800/688-6896	Thomas F. White SF, CA	`www.lombard.com`	$34	$500 acct. min.

Continued

Table 12-1 Continued

Service/800#	Parent Company	URL/other	Minimum Commission	Comments
Max Ule's Tickerscreen	Herzog, Heine Geuld, Inc.	Compuserve ('82)	20% discount	No Web trading.
National Discount Brokers 800/888-3999	Sherwood Securities Jersey City, NJ	pawws.secapl.com/ndb Compuserve	$28 (Less $8 for NASDAQ trades)	$1000 acct. min; Deal w/ Compuserve.
The Net Investor 800/NET-4250	Howe Barnes Chicago, IL	pawws.secapl.com/ to 3k, 1.5 cents over	$29 + 2.5 cents/sh	$5000 acct. min.
PC Financial Network 800/TALK-PCF	Pershing unit of DLJ Jersey City, NJ	www.pcfn.com AOL; Prodigy; Wow!; Reuters	$40	100 free real time quotes per trade.
QuickWay Plus 800/837-7220	Quick & Reilly	AOL, CompuServe ('86)	$37.50	Software package.
WealthWebK. 800/368-3668	Aufhauser NY, NY	www.aufhauser.com	$34 up to 1700 shs	10% off PC trades.
Vanguard Brokerage 800/992-8327	Vanguard Group	www.vanguard.com	contact for rates	Competitive, *Please check for current rates and policies.

—Sources: Jupiter Communications, and the companies themselves.

Full-Service Brokerage Sites

✳ Goldman Sachs www.gs.com

Content 📖 *Presentation* ☺☺☺ *Overall* 👍👍

This looks like a career opportunity center. There's nothing here for individual investors; it's geared toward Goldman's institutional clients (and probably toward its CEO).

✳ Gruntal & Co. www.gruntal.com

Content 📖📖📖 *Presentation* ☺☺ *Overall* 👍👍

Some nice stuff may be found here, including an investment newsletter, market commentary, research reports, and a monthly economic calendar. It also has a limited list of links to other financial Web sites.

✳ Hambrecht & Quist www.hamquist.com

Content 📖📖📖 *Presentation* ☺☺☺ *Overall* 👍👍👍

Due to H&Q's heavy ties to the Silicon Valley technology community, this site should be one to watch in the future for research and new Website developments. This company was responsible for taking many of the players on the Internet public, including Netscape Communications, CyberCash, and E*Trade.

✳ Kemper
networth.galt.com/www/home/mutual/
kempercash (Money Fund)

Content 📖📖📖📖 *Presentation* ☺☺☺☺ *Overall* 👍👍👍👍

Kemper's site is nicely done, and their second URL is for Kemper Money Market Funds only.

www.kemper.com

✳ Legg Mason www.leggmason.com

Content 📖📖📖📖📖 *Presentation* ☺☺☺☺☺ *Overall* 👍👍👍👍👍

This site is indeed impressive. Nice features of this site include a graphical map, a well-organized index, daily market commentary, and lots of investment planning tools. Their mutual funds are very good overall, too. Curious investors will probably want to take a glance at this site, especially if you're a shareholder in a Legg Mason fund.

✳ Merrill Lynch www.ml.com

Content 📖📖📖 *Presentation* ☺☺☺ *Overall* 👍👍👍

Merrill Lynch's Internet site is very well done, as you would expect from the largest brokerage firm in the world. Its state-of-the-art areas focus on four key topics:

- Investor Learning Center contains investment basics.

- Personal Finance Center has several excellent planning tools to help you map out things like financing college or choosing a mortgage.

- Business Planning Center shows small businesses how to deal with areas such as employee benefits and obtaining financing.

- Financial News & Research Center contains key market indicators and commentary.

The site also contains several Real Audio clips, information about Merrill Lynch, and e-mail. However, the articles tend to be slightly dated, so investors should probably seek their market and economic data elsewhere.

✳ Morgan Stanley www.ms.com

Content 📖📖 *Presentation* ☺☺☺ *Overall* 👌👌

This site is geared toward potential corporate and investment banking clients. It does, however, have a couple of things of interest for small investors. International and emerging markets indexes may be found here; its MSCI EAFE Index (Morgan Stanley Capital International's Europe, Australia, Far East) is the main benchmark for judging international funds.

✳ Prudential Securities
www.prusec.com

Content 📖📖📖 *Presentation* ☺☺☺☺ *Overall* 👌👌👌👌

To its credit, Prudential was the first traditional (i.e., full-service) brokerage to offer its customers the ability to review account information and to e-mail brokers. But don't expect trading any time soon (though account access should be added).

Finally, Prudential also has a co-branding agreement with AT&T's WorldNet service and Netscape's browser, offering a customized package to clients. Investors should contact their brokers for information.

✳ Smith Barney
www.nestegg.iddis.com/smithbarney

Content 📖📖 *Presentation* ☺☺☺☺ *Overall* 👌👌👌

This site was built the old-fashioned way, too. Although snazzy and with a lot of nice graphics, it offers little in the way of direct investment advice.

Part V

Fund & Investment Web Resources

We now move into the general fund resources section. The news and fund company sites are bigger and better than these offerings, due to their deep-pocketed parentage. But some of these smaller, general investment sites do have a lot to offer. Plus, there are several premium investment services that are worth considering, especially for serious investors. I'll review and discuss each of these in Part V. Although I've left many sites out, I strongly believe that you'll be able to find all the information you need in the sites covered.

In Chapter 13, I focus on the big information and market data sites, like Reuters Money Network, The Syndicate, and Thomson Financial. Some of these are pay services, but most are free. Don't worry; even with those that charge, I'll steer you to the best deals available. Though I couldn't spare as much space as I'd have liked for some of these offerings due to the sheer number of sites out there, I concentrate on my favorites.

Finally, Chapter 14 covers resources for personal finance, banking, taxes, and other topics only tangentially related to investing and mutual funds. Highlights include the SEC's EDGAR Web page and other government data sources, plus a look at Bank Rate Monitor (bank and CD rates) and IBC Financial Data (money fund data—

okay, I admit, I'm a little partial). After reading through these chapters, you should at least have an excellent idea of what types of information are available and where to begin your hunt.

13

Information on Funds and Investing

Even though there is enough information available under the no-load fund group's sites to keep you reading for half a century, you must remember that most are still trying to sell you their funds (or sell you something). So, with this in mind, we begin our review of general financial sites—those without a particular fund or product bias (though they all, of course, have some sort of bias). Though most of these are smaller operations, with far fewer resources, there are plenty of hidden jewels.

I list these in order of preference. But I also must say that every single site listed here has at least some useful function (otherwise it didn't make the cut).

Recommended Fund and Investment Sites

Many of these sites cater to advanced investors, but I try to balance these with plenty of basic Websites.

✳ INVESTools (by Tabula Interactive) investools.com

Content 📖📖📖📖📖 *Presentation* ☺☺☺☺☺ *Overall* 👍👍👍👍👍

Privately-held Tabula Interactive of San Francisco runs the INVESTools site, which features a tremendous amount of helpful information. Fund reports from Morningstar, the premier fund-ranking company, are available here for a $5.00 fee—using CyberCash and secure browsers. Morningstar says that the requests for Internet access to these reports has been overwhelming. INVESTools was the first site to feature these reports, though others, notably Galt's NETWorth, have added this feature.

Laird Foshay, president of Tabula Interactive, says, "The Web audience and infrastructure have finally reached a point where major information providers such as Morningstar are excited about offering their services on the Internet. This is especially true for investment services because the customers are more affluent, more wired, and more ready to participate in an online economy."

Overall, the site is tremendous. Though some of the research, news, and newsletters available will cost you, the site has enough free information that you don't need to pay for anything. Of course, the fees are reasonable for the products that do cost money.

Of particular interest to heavy 'Net users is the *Investors' Web Watch*, written by John Brobst of INVESTools. This "guide to investing with the Internet on the installment plan" contains well-written articles on investing on the Internet. Well done.

✳ Mutual Funds Interactive
www.brill.com

Content 📖📖📖📖📖 *Presentation* ☺☺☺ *Overall* 💧💧💧💧💧

Known as *the* Mutual Funds Home Page, this site is one of the best out there. Marla Brill, a freelance writer who specializes in mutual funds, is the brains behind this site (she has ties to Dalbar, publisher of *Mutual Fund Market News*, an industry weekly). Features include: Funds 101, a primer on fund investing; Fund Profiles; articles on funds galore; and one of the few *moderated* newsgroups on funds.

This is perhaps the best site devoted solely to mutual funds on the Net. Articles are updated approximately weekly, but this frequency may increase as more editorial staff members are added. It also contains a host of helpful links to other fund-related sites.

✳ Nest Egg Magazine
nestegg.iddis.com

Content 📖📖📖📖📖 *Presentation* ☺☺☺ *Overall* 🌢🌢🌢🌢

This site was done by IDD Information Services, publisher of *Investment Dealers' Digest*, which also runs the *Barron's* magazine site. Its Tradeline Mutual Fund Center contains minimal fund data, and there is a lot of information on individual stocks. However, its links to the New York Finance Institute and its index are excellent features. Also, articles from *Nest Egg* magazine add to the usable material. This is definitely a site worth checking in on.

IDD's Web-Finance (`nestegg.iddis.com/WebFinance`) has great coverage of the Internet investment industry, and it has a very well-done link section (Gateways). Its introduction states, "We're not for everyone. If you're looking for the latest stock rumor, try one of those newsgroups. Want a free stock quote? You're in the wrong place."

✳ Mutual Fund Education Alliance
www.mfea.com

Content 📖📖📖📖 *Presentation* ☺☺☺☺ *Overall* 🌢🌢🌢🌢

This new no-load fund haven has one of the best collections of educational material on the Web. Features include: pages and performance on over 1,000 funds, search and planning programs, and literature galore.

✳ InvestorGuide www.investorguide.com

Content 📖📖📖📖 *Presentation* ☺☺☺ *Overall* 🔥🔥🔥

Yet a third IDD site, this area contains one of the best compilations of links available. Also, it contains personal finance topics galore, news and market data, and much more. While its interface leaves something to be desired, it's easy enough to find your way around once you've been there for a couple of minutes.

✳ Quicken Financial Network www.qfn.com

Content 📖📖📖📖 *Presentation* ☺☺☺☺ *Overall* 🔥🔥🔥🔥

This personal finance mega-site is slightly out of place here, but it's so large that it demands attention early. The network contains four other areas in addition to the investing section, NETWorth, which we reviewed in Chapter 11. Quicken Financial Network also has investing resources of its own. Its main areas are Insurance, Banking, Reference, and Information and News.

Insurance

Several companies are represented in this fast-developing section (Lincoln Benefit Life, MetLife, TIG, and Zurich Direct), and more are being added by the month. Interactive

Insurance Service was recently acquired by Quicken; it features home, life, car, and other insurance types.

Banking

Compass, CoreStates, Home Savings of America, Smith Barney, Travelers, US Bank, and Wells Fargo are just some of the partners with Quicken in this electronic banking section.

Reference

This area contains the electric library from Infonautics and more.

Information and News

Individual Inc. provides news for this piece. Even though it is a little thin, it is conveniently located.

Quicken users have access to this site loaded into recent editions of their software, so they should be familiar with some of QFN's features.

BankNow on AOL

Quicken unveiled a new service (downloadable free) on AOL in August 1996 for home banking. The simplified interface is nice, and BankNow gives RSA 1,024-bit security access to checking, savings, credit card, and money market accounts. Once Intuit has mastered the nuances of online banking on AOL, expect it to roll out some of the same features at **www.qfn.com** in the coming months.

Finally, Intuit also offers Investor Insight (**http://www.investorinsight.com**), a pay service that offers: downloads of news stories, five-year price histories for stocks, charts of price performance reports, and personalized reports "that provide an overview of all your investments." Other options are ordering company reports online and creating custom indexes of stock groups or fund groups.

✳ Mutual Fund Research www.webcom.com/fundlink

Content 📖 *Presentation* ☺☺ *Overall* 👌

This is a nice site, one that contains top-performing funds, fund news, an introduction to mutual funds, and a few other things. Unfortunately, much of the information is extremely outdated. But you might want to check in just to see if it has finally gotten its act together.

✳ IBC Financial Data www.ibcdata.com

Content 📖📖📖📖 *Presentation* ☺☺☺ *Overall* 👌👌👌

I must disclose my conflict of interest upfront—I work for IBC Financial Data, Inc., so you'll have to take my review with a grain of salt. Our site, however, is *the* source for money market mutual fund yields, and our lists of the top-yielding funds (general-purpose, government- or Treasury-only, as well as tax-free) are updated weekly. These files are posted Wednesday evenings for money funds and Thursday evening for bond funds. (Yes, we have bond fund data, too.)

The information is taken from IBC Financial Data's weekly institutional publications, *Money Fund Report* and *Bond Fund Report*. Finally, our home page has posted our weekly MFR All Taxable Average 7-Day Yield, which is the most widely watched money fund average in the country.

✳ GNN's Personal Finance Center
www.gnn.com/gnn/meta/finance/

Content 📖 *Presentation* ☺☺ *Overall* 👍👍

Even though the articles here are downright bad, you might want to at least visit this site since parent America Online is sure to reinforce its content. It has links to the Webcrawler search area (discussed in Chapter 8), which does a good job of listing investment resources. I expect this site to get better in the near future. Until then, though, go elsewhere.

Premium Services

✳ Thomson MarketEdge ($)
www.marketedge.com

Content 📖📖 *Presentation* ☺☺ *Overall* 👆👆👆

MarketEdge costs $7.95 a month, but it is one of the more useful and readable information sources on the Internet. However, more and more features are showing up in the free area. Thomson has been out in force on the Web. (It provides data and services for many other sites, including news for Fidelity's @82DEV Web feature).

Features include Market Monitor, a daily online newsletter, portfolio tracking, alerts and quotes, reports on stocks and funds, earnings forecasts, performance rankings, and screening features. A free 30-day trial offer is available. Although many investors will want to subscribe to this service, less active traders can find most of this data for free elsewhere.

MarketEdge Navigator is the place to go to get an overview of the Thomson site. Its features include: Market Monitor, Stock Research, Fund Research, Bond Research, Bulletin Boards, Talk to MarketEdge, and Utilities.

Market Monitor

This area lists earnings surprises, a weekly economic calendar, an industry journal, mergers and acquisitions, news on the economy, stories on tech stocks, and news on the debt markets.

Stock/Bond Research

If you are one to invest in individual securities, there's plenty here. But most could probably be gotten free elsewhere.

Fund Research

Fund Reports; Top Performers; Investment Flows; Fund Screen; Fund Alerts; Statistical Spotlight; Current Fund Quotes; The Month in Review; Industry Digest are all included in this area.

Municipal Bond Research Center

Regional Review; Municipal Bond Guide; Bulletin Boards; and, finally, MarketEdge are included in this area; they contain options for Member Utilities and an area for Frequently Asked Questions.

✳ Reuters Money Network ($)
www.rmn.com

Content 📖📖📖 *Presentation* ☺☺☺ *Overall* 🔥🔥🔥

Previously, this service was available only through a proprietary bulletin board service and software, but it has since been revamped for the Internet. The site, which has a "basic" and "premium" fee structure, was created by Reality Technologies "combining powerful investment software with a complete array of online financial information, news, and data."

Though expensive, this is one of the few products to combine software and data functions. It features portfolio updates, Morningstar data and reports, and much more. But all-in-all, you can get most of the information free elsewhere. It contains many of the same features as Thomson MarketEdge, so I won't list them again. You may want to visit just to see if they've stopped charging for the service.

Other Sites

✳ Briefing (by Charter Media)
www.briefing.com

Content 📖📖📖📖 *Presentation* ☺☺ *Overall* 👆👆👆

This site is for more advanced investors, but it is an excellent resource. It's one of the best sites anywhere for obtaining economic data (if you're so inclined). Briefing is run by Richard C. Green, who must be independently wealthy to be giving away such excellent and timely data (actually, he is planning on initiating a subscription fee). When economic news breaks, Briefing is ahead of almost every other major media outlet in updating its information and commentary. It also now has quotes (like everyone else in the universe).

The organization that runs it, Charter Media, say the site "provides valuable, useable market information to help you make money in the markets. Briefing provides information to help you make informed investment and trading decisions. Updates are posted throughout the day as developments occur."

My favorite feature is its economic calendar. Not only does it gives estimates of the numbers prior to their release, it also gives the market's response to the data mere minutes after the number is announced.

✳ Bulletproof's Wall Street Web
www.bulletproof.com

Content 📖📖 *Presentation* ☺☺☺☺ *Overall* 👍👍👍

This site is on the cutting edge of technology. It has instant quotes, searches, personalized securities lists, portfolio management, charting, and more. Many of the services cost money, but advanced investors will probably want to check in here and see what's brewing.

✳ DBC (Data Broadcast Corp.)
www.dbc.com

Content 📖📖📖📖 *Presentation* ☺☺☺☺ *Overall* 👍👍👍👍

As mentioned previously, Data Broadcasting, maker of the Signal FM broadcasting stock price service, has an extensive Website. Of course, it has quotes galore, but it also has become a force in up-to-date (close to real-time) news, including a page on Internet technology stories. It also has many premium packages for professionals (or info-addicts).

Although DBC has data galore, it sometimes can even be too much. For the technically inclined, however, this site is hard to beat for raw data.

✳ The Finance Center www.tfc.com

Content 📖📖📖 *Presentation* ☺☺☺ *Overall* 👍👍👍

This site has plenty of links and ties to investment newsletters. There's a lot of good stuff, but I'd limit my time here. It is run by Florida-based Pinson & Associates.

✳ The Syndicate
www.moneypages.com/syndicate/

Content 📖📖 *Presentation* ☺☺☺ *Overall* 👍👍👍

The Syndicate was one of the first popular independent investment advice sites on the Web, but recently it has languished. **Moneypages.com** is the host for the Syndicate site, which has an extensive list of financial links and several other resources of note. News from Individual Inc.'s NewsPage and DBC Online is available, as are several good articles under the Stocks section. Finally, the mutual funds section leads to the official home page for the **misc.invest.funds** FAQ. Visit, but don't spend too much time.

✳ Telescan's Wall Street City
www.wallstreetcity.com

Content 📖📖 *Presentation* ☺☺☺☺ *Overall* 👍👍👍

Wall Street City looks impressive, but for now it is merely an expensive marketing tool for parent Telescan's software. However, the site clearly expects to be here in the future, so perhaps some more rational investment advice will come calling. Until then, investors may want to stop in every once in a while to admire the graphics.

Telescan, maker of technical analysis software, says in its release about its super-site, "Wall Street City contains more than just the basics of quotes, news and fundamentals … it also gives users access to educational tools, discussion groups, banks and brokers, who can help them make more profitable investment decisions." While this is overstating it a little bit, the site will be one to watch if it can sign up some additional outside information providers.

The site's "districts" include: Mutual Fund Tower, Research District, Wall Street Pub (chat), News Room, and more. Nifty extras include the ability to create your own custom Java ticker-tape and access to Telescan Investor's Platform (TIPNet), for more advanced technical screening tools.

Telescan and Wall Street City are geared toward traders and speculators. Most fund investors will want to evaluate the information given carefully. On another note: Telescan CEO David L. Brown has his own competing text, *Cyber Investing: Cracking Wall Street with Your Personal Computer*, which is mainly an overview of technical software in the guise of a book on the Internet.

Other Sites on Funds

✳ FinanceHub www.financehub.com

Content 📖📖 *Presentation* ☺☺ *Overall* 👍👍

This site, designed by Web designer InterSoft Solutions of Florida, contains link lists on venture capital, banks, investments, stock market, commerce, and legal.

✳ Research (Magazine) www.researchmag.com

Content 📖📖📖 *Presentation* ☺☺ *Overall* 👍👍

Though this site is meant more for journalists and investment professionals, it contains in-depth stories and lots of links. Its four sections include: Online Magazine; Investor Net—pages and pages of investment information, though mainly on individual companies; Broker Net; and Institution Net. Quotes, company briefs, and charts are also all provided for free. (I mentioned this in Chapter 9, News, site as well.)

✳ Stock Smart www.stocksmart.com

Content 📖📖📖📖 *Presentation* ☺☺☺ *Overall* 👍👍👍👍

This site contains earnings estimates, quotes, and a few other nice features. It is for individual stock investors primarily. This site could develop into a major center, though, due to its extensive information. It has lots and lots of mutual fund data, including performance and statistics on more than 5,000 funds. I couldn't figure out who these guys were, but boy do they know how to handle their technology.

✳ The Investor's Edge www.irnet.com

Content 📖📖 *Presentation* ☺ *Overall* 👍👍

This site's main benefit is information on individual companies, which pay to have investor relations materials listed here. There is mutual fund price data, but little else to interest the fund investor. However, because Microsoft has begun using it as an information source, I'm sure we'll be seeing it around. The site was undergoing a tremendous amount of changes, and it was trying to mold itself into an investment super-site when I last checked.

✳ FundScape www.fundscape.com

Content 📖📖 *Presentation* ☺☺ *Overall* 👍👍

This site's main strength is its performance tracker, which is geared toward stockbrokers and financial planners. As a matter of fact, the entire site is geared toward brokers and planners, so individual investors should steer clear (lest ye be hit by brokers' marketing pitches!).

✳ Mutual Fund Café www.mfcafe.com

Content 📖📖 *Presentation* ☺☺ *Overall* 🖐🖐

Though this site is meant more for journalists and investment professionals, it contains some interesting information, such as sales trends, regulatory issues, and articles.

✳ Bonds Online www.bondsonline.com

Content 📖📖 *Presentation* ☺☺ *Overall* 🖐🖐🖐

Visit this site if you really like bonds. This site and the following site appear to be run by individuals (as are many of these "second-tier" listings).

✳ Money Talks www.talks.com

Content 📖 *Presentation* ☺ *Overall* 🖐

This smaller site has weekly columns that aren't too exciting.

✷ 1-800-Mutuals
www.1800mutuals.com

Content 📖 *Presentation* ☺☺ *Overall* ♦

This Dallas stockbroker firm has opened a site meant for fund investors, but investors are advised to seek information and trading services elsewhere. Even though the site is worth a visit, the fees charged clearly make fund buying too expensive here.

Features include contests (they're giving away $1 million, payable over 20 years) and fund reports from CDA/Wiesenberger.

Quotes and Information on Stocks

We've seen plenty of sites that provide quotes. Many have used secondary providers, some of which are listed below. As I briefly mentioned, all of the Internet quote providers have involved primarily delayed quotes (20 minutes or more). What are referred to as "real-time" quotes are either up-to-the-minute or up-to-the-second prices, and they normally cost a good bit of money (delayed quotes are practically free on the Internet).

The following sites all provide delayed quotes, and most also offer a premium service for real-time quotes. Prices vary, but most are $20-30 a month. There are, of course, myriad other ways of getting premium quotes—via FM radio waves, cable, and satellite delivery. These and other high-end providers will surely be forced to cut their prices due to cheaper Internet competitors.

✳ PC Quote www.pcquote.com

Content 📖📖📖📖 *Presentation* ☺☺☺ *Overall* 👍👍👍

This site, and the following sites, gives fund and stock quotes, as do many others on the Web. For quotes, PC Quote is one of the best.

✳ QuoteCom www.quote.com

Content 📖📖📖 *Presentation* ☺☺☺ *Overall* 👍👍👍

This company provides quotes to other servers, and it has both free delayed and pay real-time quotes available. This is the best of the quote providers, in my opinion. (Beware, there is an imposter site, www.quotecom.com!)

✳ Wall St. Online   www.wso.com

Content 📖📖 *Presentation* ☺☺☺ *Overall* 👍👍

This site is primarily for stock investors, too. I wouldn't trust the advice here as far as I could through my monitor. Unless you'd like to visit every investment site available, don't bother with this one.

✳ Motley Fool   fool.web.aol.com

Content 📖📖📖 *Presentation* ☺☺ *Overall* 👍👍

Fools David and Tom Gardner have now expanded beyond America Online to establish a stock-picking site on the Web. While I advise against individual stocks and some of their picks in particular (I became a little suspicious when they recommended AOL itself, their employer), there are pieces of sound investment advice here.

There has been talk of the Gardner brothers leaving AOL's wing to go it on their own (solely on the Internet), but this hasn't happened as of yet. Due to their lack of fund information, I recommend that investors steer clear.

✳ Netstockdirect
www.netstockdirect.com

Content 📖📖📖 *Presentation* ☺☺☺ *Overall* 👍👍👍

This Web page contains information on companies that have dividend reinvestment programs (DRIPs). If you are tempted to buy individual stocks, buying directly from the companies themselves is the way to go—bypassing the broker's commission. Companies that have direct-investment programs normally also allow for the reinvestment of dividends and the purchase of additional shares.

✳ Silicon Investor
www.techstocks.com

Content 📖📖📖 *Presentation* ☺☺☺☺ *Overall* 👍👍👍👍

This site, along with Motley Fool, the newsgroup **misc.invest.stocks,** and others, has been in the thick of some of the hottest technology stock stories around. While the SEC hasn't accused anyone here of intentional manipulation, these sites have become magnets for brokers who try to talk up their picks. Avoid these sites. If you must invest, be sure that the individual stocks you own make up only a fraction of your investments. The charts here are very nice.

✴ Stockmaster
www.stockmaster.com

Content 📖📖📖 *Presentation* ☺☺ *Overall* 👍👍👍

This site, formerly run by the MIT AI (artificial intelligence) lab, provides charts for mutual funds and stocks. Unfortunately, they don't adjust for distributions. So, if you have a large payout, as Magellan did in 1995, the chart is ruined. For this reason, you're better off looking elsewhere.

✴ Equis www.equis.com

Content 📖 *Presentation* ☺ *Overall* 👍

This is a Reuters subsidiary that specializes in technical analysis, or charting, software and market data. Its main purpose is an ad for the product, which I'm not too crazy about.

14

Personal Finance Resources

This chapter focuses on Web resources that are peripherally related to investing: economics, banking (with bank-sponsored funds listed here), taxes, government resources, insurance, and more. While I don't have space to cover everything in as much depth as I would like, I believe that the sites provided are among the best of the non-investment areas, but I'm purposefully omitting many more excellent sites in these disciplines. (Perhaps another book will cover them in more detail.)

This is the final of my "review chapters" where I concentrate on the Websites themselves. I breeze through banks, taxes, economics, and insurance, then end with a listing of a few miscellaneous sites. In the next chapter, I return to the heavy text format, taking on online buying and selling. Finally, in Chapter 16 I will talk about security, regulations, and digital dangers and end with an addendum on the future (which will be the present by the time you're reading it, I hope).

Banking

After investing, online banking holds the most promise once the Internet has taken over the world. The ability to check balances online beats a voice mail system, and once online bill paying takes off you'll begin to get excited. The banks below represent just a small subset of those on the Internet, but they represent the cutting edge. Check these sites out first, but also look for your local, own, or favorite bank online, too.

The sites below are a smorgasbord of choices; I emphasize some for their ground-breaking no-fee Internet sites, some for their mutual funds, and some for their technology prowess. While I stress one thing or another, most will have a lot of the same services and areas.

✳ Bank Rate Monitor www.brm.com

Content 📖📖📖📖 *Presentation* ☺☺☺ *Overall* 🍷🍷🍷

Infobank is the title of Bank Rate Monitor's site, which has consumer savings and other bank rates. Its MMDA—money market deposit account—and CD averages are widely quoted. Banking-related articles from *Bank Rate Monitor* and its other publications, such as *100 Highest Yields*, may be found here, as well as lots of data on high-yielding bank products.

Of course, what you'd want with a bank product, I wouldn't know because money market *mutual funds* yield on average almost 2 percent higher. But definitely give this site a look, especially if you insist on insurance and are in the market for a certificate of deposit. CDs normally are competitive with money funds, while other types of accounts are not.

✳ Security First National Bank
www.sfnb.com

Content 📖📖📖📖 *Presentation* ☺☺☺☺☺ *Overall* 👍👍👍👍

This little company made big news as the first truly online bank. An Atlanta company, it exists only on the Internet. Don't worry that it is a fly-by-night operation, however; its parents include several big banks (Wachovia Savings Bank, Cardinal Bankshares, and Huntington Bankshares).

Even though its checking is free, I'd suggest waiting for your regional bank to join the party before banking on the Internet. Its CD rates and fees are extremely competitive. The site is very well done though.

✴ First Chicago NBD

Content 📖📖📖📖 *Presentation* ☺☺☺☺ *Overall* 👍👍👍

This bank began imposing a fee of $3 for using a teller for routine tasks over a year ago, and it has since seen the number of people using electronic transactions rise to half of its customers. The company is usually on the cutting edge of technology and transaction processing. This is a good example of a big corporate bank's site.

✴ Bank of America www.bankamerica.com

Content 📖📖📖📖📖 *Presentation* ☺☺☺☺☺ *Overall* 👍👍👍👍

BofA's home page will blow you away with its graphics and features. It is one of the most extensive bank sites I've seen. BofA is a leader in home banking, and most everything else. Definitely pay it a visit and look around.

✴ J. P. Morgan www.jpmorgan.com

Content 📖📖📖 *Presentation* ☺☺☺ *Overall* 👍👍👍👍

For some mysterious reason, J. P. Morgan has been at the forefront of warning about the "Year 2000 Problem"—when computers are supposed to go haywire because they can only handle two-digit dates. The site is for institutional clients or the curious, but fund investors should look elsewhere.

Bank-Owned and Other Financial Company Fund Group Sites

Even though many of the companies below also have banking features, I concentrate on their mutual fund sections. Banks have been aggressively defending their turf from the mutual fund groups, but they've found that their best weapon has been to join them.

As regulatory barriers have fallen, banks have started, purchased, and merged their own mutual fund offerings. While these were primarily money market mutual funds at first, a handful of banks have built well-rounded, top performing fund groupings. I list the biggest and the best of these below:

✳ Fleet (Galaxy Funds) www.fleet.com

Content 📖📖📖📖 *Presentation* ☺☺☺☺ *Overall* ♦♦♦♦♦

Fleet was early with a feature called the Personal Navigator, "your own personal site on the Internet." Its site contains several areas: About You is the personal finance section, containing articles, calculators, and budget planner; Personal Banking Products and Services contains the information on

Fleet's mutual funds. The fund area contains an Investment Allocation Analyzer, which recommends fund percent for the data you enter; the site also contains:Business *Banking and About Fleet.*

Overall, the educational material is very good and quite readable. The Galaxy family of mutual funds offers a wide and competitive selection. Investors in the New England area (or perhaps soon anywhere) should look into the plans that link checking and fund accounts at this site.

✳ NationsBank www.nationsbank.com

Content 📖📖📖📖 *Presentation* ☺☺☺ *Overall* 👍👍👍👍

Information on NationsBank's fund family may be found under the Personal section. It has a diversified family of funds, plus PC banking and plenty of other goodies. Look for this bank to expand its presence aggressively on the Internet, since its Chairman Hugh McColl, has become a recent convert to the technology.

✳ PNCBank's Compass Capital Funds www.compassfunds.com

Content 📖📖📖 *Presentation* ☺☺☺ *Overall* 👍👍👍

"What differentiates our Web site from most others is the ability to access information immediately without the need to scroll through one Web page after another," says Compass Capital President Karen Sabath. Indeed, the site has done a good job at making fund information—composition, holdings, performance, ratings, NAVs (daily and historic), expenses, and a summary—dynamically available.

✳ Wells Fargo (Stagecoach Funds) www.wellsfargo.com

Content 📖📖📖📖📖 *Presentation* ☺☺☺☺☺ *Overall* 💧💧💧💧

It looks as if Wells Fargo and BankAmerica are having a showdown. These two San Francisco banks are competing for the best bank site. Wells Fargo has a tiny technological edge; its site has the latest bells and whistles. It also, of course, offers banking, mutual funds through several proprietary fund families, and online account access.

Taxes

✳ Internal Revenue Service www.irs.ustreas.gov

Content 📖📖📖📖📖 *Presentation* ☺☺☺ *Overall* 💧💧💧

Any form you could possibly need may be found here (`http://www.irs.ustreas.gov/prod/forms_pubs/forms.html`). You'll also have to download Adobe's ubiquitous Acrobat reader to view and print them if you don't have it already, but once that's done downloading is a snap. Their introductory newsletter is nice, too. But don't forget it's the IRS whose site you're on.

✳ Internal Revenue Code mip.upstlse.fr/ ~grundman/ustax/www/contents

This is an index of the entire tax code; for the insane (or tax accountants) only!

Miscellaneous Other Tax-Related Sites

✳ AICPA www.rutgers.edu/Accounting/raw/aicpa/ home

✴ American Bar Association Tax
Section www.abanet/org/tax/home

✴ NetTaxes Page www.ypn.com/taxes

✴ Intuit's TurboTax Online
www.intuit.com/turbotax

Government Sites

Although the government generally can be counted on to
be 10 years behind the times in practically every field of
technology, it's been a pleasant surprise seeing some of
their Web sites. Several are even on the cutting edge. As
more and more government resources go online, the usefulness of the sites that follow will expand dramatically.

✳ EDGAR (SEC)
www.town.hall.org/edgar/edgar.html

Content 📖 *Presentation* ☺ *Overall* 👍👍

The Securities and Exchange Commission's EDGAR site (Electronic Data Gathering, Analysis and Retrieval system) offers investors several important functions. First, financial information for every major U.S. corporation is filed here and made available the following day. Electronic SEC filings include financial statements (the most important of which are Form 10K, the annual company financials, and Form 10Q, quarterly balance sheet statements), registrations, tender offers, and more.

Mutual fund information available on EDGAR is there, but it might take you awhile to find it. The SEC's site debuted in September 1995, and it quickly became one of the most accessed areas of the Web. Over 100,000 hits per day are being reported, as investors peruse corporate and regulatory filings.

There is also an alternative EDGAR site at New York University (http://edgar.stern.nyu.edu) that mirrors the SEC's site. EDGAR data still is released only after at least 24 hours, so private services, such as Lexis-Nexis, Dow Jones, Disclosure, and Bloomberg still have a market for their up-to-the-minute private services. However, this may change in the future. Cheaper services, including EDGAR Online and SEC-Live, are also available.

While EDGAR leaves much to be desired, several private companies can make accessing the EDGAR database slightly less daunting. Most of these charge for their information, so I do not recommend using them. But if you're considering purchasing an individual company, it might make sense to use one of these services to check its filings.

EDGAR Alternatives (Private Companies)

✳ Disclosure ($) www.disclosure.com

Content 📖📖📖📖 *Presentation* ☺☺☺ *Overall* 👌👌👌

Available at its Website, and through IBM's infoMarket service, Disclosure,Inc., offers several packages for accessing its extensive SEC database of company data. Over 12,000 U.S. publicly traded companies are available, with information gleaned from both SEC filings and annual reports. IBM's "cryptolope" security technology is being used to provide packaging for secure transactions. (There are other EDGAR sorters that are not listed here.)

✳ U.S. Treasury www.ustreas.gov/treasury

Content 📖📖📖📖 *Presentation* ☺☺ *Overall* 👌👌👌

There's plenty of useful stuff at this location. In addition to speeches and articles, a useful area at the U.S. Treasury is its Series EE Savings Bonds section, which may be found in the Bureau of Public Debt area. Fifteen million Americans a year purchase bonds directly through the Treasury, and much of this will potentially be shifted onto electronic media. For now, though, there's plenty of information about savings bonds, so investors may find it useful to visit here.

Though the Treasury doesn't plan to move the larger, $3+ trillion dollar bond auctions onto the Net, tremendous pressure may well force it to offer these larger-denomination ($1,000 or $10,000) government bonds directly to investors.

Other bureaus with areas inside the extensive Treasury domain include: Internal Revenue Service, Customs Service, Bureau of Alcohol, Tobacco, and Firearms, Financial Management Service, United States Secret Service, Office of Thrift Supervision, United States Mint, Office of the Comptroller of the Currency, Bureau of Public Debt, and Bureau of Engraving and Printing.

✳ U.S. Department of Commerce
www.doc.gov

Content 📖📖📖📖 *Presentation* ☺☺☺☺ *Overall* 👍👍👍

Commerce, too, has a lot more agencies than you probably would have guessed. (Check out: `http://www.doc.gov/agencies.html`). There's enough stuff here to keep you busy for a good week, but it can be tough going through the layers.

✳ Commerce Dept.'s Stat USA Site ($) www.stat-usa.gov

Content 📖📖📖📖 *Presentation* ☺☺☺☺ *Overall* 👍👍👍👍

This page, run by the Department of Commerce, has an extensive collection of economic statistics, but it costs $150 a year to access most of the economic and trade data. It's well organized, though, and contains tons of information. If you need GDP numbers, housing starts, personal income, and other statistics, you can probably get the raw data here.

The following government site also has a collection of economic data:

✳ U.S. Department of Labor www.dol.gov

✳ "Thomas" U.S. Congress thomas.loc.gov

Content 📖📖📖 *Presentation* ☺☺☺ *Overall* 👍👍👍

For updates on recent legislation, this is the place. It also has plenty of links to other government sites.

✳ U.S. Postal Service Scam Tips

www.usps.gov/websites/depart/inspect

Content 📖📖📖📖 *Presentation* ☺☺☺☺☺ *Overall* ♦♦♦♦♦

The postal service has a good area on scam detection, which anyone unsure of a solicitation should consult.

✳ Federal Reserve of St. Louis' FRED www.stls.frb.org/fred

Content 📖📖📖📖 *Presentation* ☺☺ *Overall* ♦♦♦

FRED stands for Federal Reserve Economic Data; various interest rate, money supply, and economic numbers are available here, as are links to the rest of the Federal Reserve systems' branches. A link to the Fed's "beige book" gives investors reports on regional economic conditions across the country.

Economics

While most investors need not pay too much attention to the field of economics, many people are quite interested. Plus, much of the economic information is central to investing. For this reason, it's important at least to be aware of the field. The sites below are the most popular and largest of the economic servers, but there are countless others.

✳ FinWeb WWW Server
www.finweb.com

Content 📖📖📖📖 *Presentation* ☺☺ *Overall* 👍👍👍

FINWeb is an economics Web site managed by James R. Garven, Ph.D. It contains plenty of links to finance journals, and it is well run. This should be your first stop when seeking out information or when beginning an educational tour of economics resources.

✳ Ohio St. Finance Links
www.cob.ohio-state.edu/dept/fin/overview

Content 📖📖📖 *Presentation* ☺☺ *Overall* 👍👍

The WWW Virtual Library of Finance and Investments is run by Ohio State's finance department. This area includes "reference aids for carrying out research in finance including journals, working papers, software,and data." The amount of information referenced is extensive, but visit only if you're serious about your economics.

Insurance

Insurance surely will be affected by the Web as well. Although the big companies have sites, there hasn't yet been a brutal price war. It will come, though, once direct sellers enter the Web en masse. Jupiter Communications' senior editor Phoebe Simpson said recently in a Barron's piece, "It will be a supermarket effect with insurance online—don't be surprised if Microsoft showcases online insurance in the next few years.... Anyone with visibility and reach can showcase insurance. They're not selling it, just housing it."

Here are just a couple of sites:

✳ Best of America Variable Annuities
www.boa.com

✳ Nationwide
www.nationwide.com

Other Uses

As the world's newspaper, radio, and newscast, all rolled into one, the Web has drawn a lot of attention from those who would restrict it. Judge Stewart Dalzell, in rejecting an early attempt at regulating content, called the medium, "the telephone writ large." He went on to extoll the "chaos and cacophony of the unfettered speech." The judge finished with the comment, "The Internet deserves the very broadest possible protection from government-imposed, content-based regulation."

Part VI

Online Trading

Some of you might be disappointed with this book's promise of telling you how exactly to buy and sell funds online. The unfortunate matter of it is that the funds and companies that I recommend you trade with are only now putting up these capabilities. I can't wait—my publisher is calling. Nonetheless, I will take you through some theoretical trades and point out some of the issues involved in trading funds online. With these final two chapters, I'll attempt to address some issues and wrap up our overview of mutual fund investing on the Internet.

In addition to showing some examples of trading via the Internet, Chapter 15 will also make you aware of many of the theoretical underpinnings behind online trades and behind online investment banking. It also reviews the history and players in online investment banking, then finishes with a brief digression on Internet mutual funds (those made up of Internet companies).

Chapter 16 takes on security, regulation, including a history of schemes on the Net, and other dangers. I will reassure you about trading online, but I'll also tell you how to make your own trades secure ... and where to go for help if you ever need it.

This chapter finishes by speculating on the future on mutual funds on the Internet. It also allows me to insert some last-minute thoughts before sending *Mutual Fund Investing on the Internet* to the printer.

15

Buying and Selling Online

This division of labour, from which so many advantages are derived, is not originally the effect of any human wisdom, which foresees and intends that general opulence to which it gives occasion. It is the necessary, though very slow and gradual consequence of a certain propensity in human nature which has in view no such extensive utility; the propensity to truck, barter, and exchange one thing for another. ... As it is the power of exchanging that gives occasion to the division of labour, so the extent of this division must always be limited by the extent ... of the market.

— *Adam Smith*, The Wealth of Nations

The market has indeed exploded, Mr. Smith. All the world's a marketplace, and we are merely traders.

—Mutual Fund Investing on the Internet

While we've already mentioned trading along with many of the fund company sites in Part IV, this chapter will discuss some of more particular aspects of buying and selling shares online. How placing trades differs from punching an order into a telephone is not easily apparent at first, but there are crucial differences that I'll explain. I also use this chapter to chronicle the budding area of investment banking-direct— the selling of shares directly to the public, with no commission, via the Internet.

As I said early in the book, the reason electronic investing is such a big deal is twofold: It cuts down on the number of errors—because the software has many built-in checks and because of the ease of record-keeping; it is cheaper—because it eliminates the broker (or at least lessens his or her workload, thus making it cheaper). A single computer server may process thousands upon thousands of information requests, trades, and confirmations with even more speed and efficiency than an entire office full of workers. Barron's magazine recently quoted SEC Commissioner Steven Wallman, "I think we are going to have increased use of the Internet for all kinds of securities transactions because it is a cost-effective way of communicating and doing business."

Already, firms like Schwab and Jack White report that online trading should represent almost half of their business in the next couple of years. It is merely a matter of time before some of the more educated among these begin exploring "direct-investment" options, especially as the companies themselves move to raise capital directly. Small firms like E*Trade are already diving into the "sell side" of this burgeoning industry, while other companies have benefitted from offering their own stock directly.

The first of these companies was Spring Street Brewing, maker of Wit Beer, but there are plenty of others. Web sites have sprung up like mushrooms to try and offer direct money-raising services to small companies. IPONet, WebIPO, and, most notably, the aforementioned E*Trade are just a few companies developing alternatives to traditional investment banking and venture capital on the Internet. I list some of these Web sites, and I explore some of the major advantages (and disadvantages) these organizations have over their competitors.

Mutual Funds versus Discount Brokers

Because the regulation surrounding mutual funds is quite heavy, trading funds online doesn't have as much an advantage over traditional methods as the other functions of Web sites have. But there are still benefits. *Just keep in mind that mutual funds may only be purchased once a day, so trades placed online are effectively the same as those placed via the phone.* In other words, intraday timing doesn't matter, even if you're online.

Even though any discount brokerage that's doing enough spending on advertising for you to notice it is probably sound financially, there's never any harm in taking just a little measure of security. Though almost all firms have SIPC, Securities

Investors Protection Corp., insurance for up to $1 million, I'd still suggest sticking with the soundest companies.

Some day soon you'll be able to log on, open a mutual fund or brokerage account, log onto to your bank's Website, transfer funds, and place trades all in the same minute, but this isn't the case as of yet. You can download the account application forms and later place the trades, but the money must be mailed to the account. The account must already have the funds in it, which is already the status quo with mutual funds—unlike brokerage accounts, you can't place the trade and get the money to them in three days.

Nonetheless, this doesn't alter the mechanics of placing the actual trade. While you can receive only the closing NAV for a fund, you are at least able to place the trade 24 hours a day. So, whenever you've made the decision to move $10,000 from your Fidelity New Millennium Fund into Fidelity Growth & Income (to make your overall portfolio more conservative, but yet still be invested in stocks), you just log on or call and place the order.

Or, on Schwab's OneSource fund network, after seeing a drop in the market you could move $1,000 from Schwab Money Market Fund (cash) into, say, Oakmark Fund to add to your stock holdings (while the adding is good). You'll have to enter an account number and a password, then enter the trading area. In Figure 15-1, I detail the information that a user must enter in order to enter a trade on Charles Schwab's mutual fund trading system:

You'll just choose buy, sell, or whatever, the amount, fund, and you'll be told if there's a transaction fee. Try out Schwab or other sites' demos to practice, just so you're aware of how quickly money can be moved.

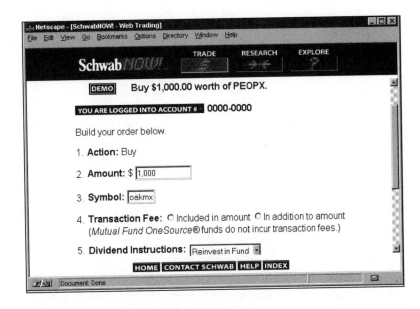

Figure 15-1. Trading is as easy as 1, 2, 3, 4, 5.

How to Invest Online

If you're going to be opening an online account, you'll want to send in a check (with an account application) for deposit into a money market fund account initially. Unless you're prepared to just pick a stock or bond fund investment with the entire investment, this way you'll be able to dollar-cost average. Most fund families have automatic monthly transfer programs, so transfer in a certain amount each month.

While you're waiting for the snail mail to deliver and turtle banking to credit your account, you can be researching investment options and strategies at various fund groups and other sites. Remember, especially on the Internet, any investment that has to be rushed, or has to be there today, is probably a bad one in the first place.

You'll discover what sort of online access is appropriate for you. Whether it is just an occasional glance at your 401(k) plan account via the Web or a nightly update of your allocations and investment news, the World Wide Web has made accessing information simple and convenient.

Investment Banking Online

The Wall Street Journal Interactive Edition reported in August 1996 that "Flamemaster Corp. (FAME) requested a 'no action' letter from the Securities and Exchange Commission to allow its stock to be traded on its World Wide Web site." In other words, they asked permission (a "no action" letter by the SEC means they won't object to your doing something, or they won't take action). Selling directly to the public is another function that the Web was made for.

Spring Street Brewing made history in 1995 as the first firm to offer its stock directly to investors on the Internet. Prospectuses were downloadable from its Web site (http://www.witbeer.com or www.interport.net/witbeer to trade Spring Street's stock), and the company raised well over $1.6 million from the sale (it's planning another offering as well). While this was all well and good, Spring Street ran into the regulators once it attempted to then set up a trading system online.

Wit-Trade was a bulletin board mechanism that listed buy and sell offers (bid and ask). Andrew Klein, president of Wit Capital Corp., has said, "Brokerage fees on the Web are coming down and will eventually near zero because the cost of each additional transaction is so miniscule." Another company that raised money early directly on the Net was PerfectData Corp.Other imitators quickly followed, including WebIPO (pictured in figure 15-2), IPO Central, and others. While many regulatory and competitive issues have yet to be worked out, it seems clear that some sort of electronic, direct-investment clearinghouse is here to stay.

SEC Commissioner Steven Wallman says, "That's fine with us. We don't care what media people use to go public. If they want to take advantage of technology, that's great." Another SEC source was quoted in *Money* magazine's online daily as saying, "The Internet is no different than any other form of advertising. But going to the market online allows companies to raise capital at lower costs, and that's good for everyone."

The Commission has also said that the use of electronic media, "enhances the efficiency of the securities market by allowing for the rapid dissemination of information to investors and financial markets in a more cost-efficient, widespread and equitable manner than the traditional paper-based methods."

The Wall Street Journal Interactive Edition also reported, "The SEC in June cleared a California company, Real Goods Trading Corp., to trade its own stock in the Internet by allowing buyers and sellers to post messages to each other."

By reducing mailing costs and other expenses, both the investor and the company raising capital may be getting better deals.

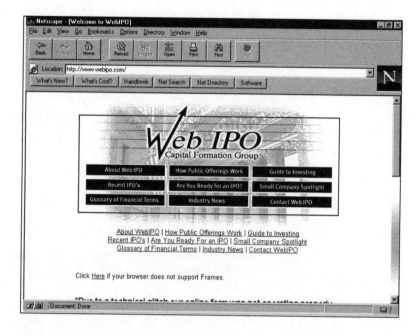

Figure 15-2. WebIPO—the second "direct investment bank" on the Internet.

Although some sticky legal and regulatory issues remain, some of which we look at in Chapter 16, it is only a matter of time before direct trading becomes a reality. Already, the area of private placements, where small groups of well-heeled investors may invest in selected ventures with almost no regulatory oversight, is a thriving business on the Web.

The Securities and Exchange Commission cleared the way in August 1996 for IPONet. A Pasadena company, W.J. Gallagher & Co., launched this service (located at www.zanax.com/iponet), which offers listings and allows purchase of private placements. Private placements are large investments made by a small number of backers, which thereby avoid most SEC requirements. This venture, and others like it, are expected to draw a lot of competition and a lot of variations as the online market matures.

Internet Mutual Funds

Of course, whenever an investment area gets "hot," a mutual fund specializing in that type of stock is sure to appear. It's also a time for investors to steer clear. If it's that hot, why do they need you to invest? Nonetheless, the Internet and interactive media funds are rolling out. Already, two are in action, and several are probably not far behind. These funds invest in Internet-related companies (which include most technology companies these days, too), such as larger players Microsoft and Netscape Communications, plus smaller companies like Macromedia and E*Trade.

The two Internet funds already available, Munder Net Fund and WWW Internet Fund, are from smaller outfits. The first is run by Munder Capital Management of Michigan, which also manages several stock funds. Munder appear to be a little slow with its Web page design, though, so I wouldn't think its knowledge of the Internet is that impressive. Munder Net and its competition below don't yet allow direct investment via the Internet, which should give you an indication of how technically-savvy the management companies are.

WWW Internet Fund (http://www.inetfund.com), on the other hand, is a startup from Lexington, Ky., which also buys all kinds of Internet-related companies. This company had the nerve to launch an Internet fund site which was still under construction! There were also links to nowhere when I visited, and the principals have never managed a mutual fund. If you're considering investing in this fund, get your head examined. Please, if you do have to invest in a fund this aggressive, at least do it through one of the larger fund groups not a fly-by-night operation.

Though it's often hard to find when investing on the 'Net, look for a company's parents or backers; they should be big. I'd suggest sticking with a broader technology funds (over 30 "technology" funds buy Internet stocks), if you must since either of these new funds (or any investing solely in Internet-related companies) will be most dangerous.

16

Security, Regulation, and Digital Dangers

We've already encountered a few questions of security, regulation and other possible roadblocks to progress on the info-investing superhighway. But I wanted to revisit several key issues, both so that you are aware of the potential dangers and so you know which are the more innocuous ones.

Already, the widespread use of automated telephone systems has brought many potential problems to the fore. But at the same time, these have been few. They've been handled quietly as well, contrary to their new online counterparts. Timothy Middleton, personal finance columnist to *The New York Times*, wrote, "The industry generally points to automated voice-response telephone systems as proof that automated transactions are no problem." Maybe, but looking at the potential dangers of online investing also points out some of the weaknesses of 800-number systems.

Sure, all this new technology is nice, but what if a computer hacker comes in and transfers my pension? And how do you know that the site you're looking at is even the "official" company site? With chats and other things involving just one individual, in particular, the possibility for misrepresentation is very real.

Fellow index fund fanatic Eric Tyson, author of *Investing for Dummies*, says, "I will echo the advice your parents gave you: Don't believe everything you read—particularly online, when you can't even identify who you're chatting with. People can disguise who they are and their motives. They can be recommending things that aren't in your best interest. This is true in the real world, too, but it's compounded online by the anonymity." Things are not always what they seem online.

Security

Certainly, the concerns voiced among news media over the past year and a half have been overwrought. Nonetheless, there are legitimate concerns that any foul play or technical error could beset your account. The regulations surrounding retirement plans in particular are myriad, but there is no insurance per se protecting 401(k) plan assets.

But retirement investors have one big new advantage from online account access: They can keep an eye on the biggest thief of this money—their employers. Employees who are aware of their account balances more often than once a quarter will be more alert to any type of fraud.

As far as a hacker breaking in and stealing plan assets, Camille Lepre, from Fidelity's FIRSCO Retirement unit, was quoted in the aforementioned *NYT* article about 401(k) security, "If there were to be an issue—and heretofore there hasn't been one—and it became clear that it was not the participant who made the transaction, we would rectify it in the participant's favor." In other words, Fidelity would make good on any losses. From public statements, the remaining largest of the fund groups would probably make the same claim, though their lawyers would undoubtedly cringe.

Jim Jubak, in the *Worth Guide to Electronic Investing*, describes an earlier "hacker episode": "In early September 1995 two Stanford University students cracked the security codes in Netscape, the most popular World Wide Web navigation software, and then published the method on the Internet itself. For days, anyone with solid computer skills had a shot at intercepting credit card numbers transmitted on the Internet in commercial transactions." Recent questions have also been raised about just how secure Microsoft's Internet Explorer really is.

The hacker story makes three important points about security on the Internet. First, there is always a way to steal anything; second, the online community is trusting (i.e., honest); and, third, commercial transactions have been going on on the Internet for some time. Thus, though there is some risk, the robust debate that occurs, and even the mischievous testing that goes on by the hackers, only strengthens future security systems.

A side note to reassure you: Netscape says "its current 128-bit encryption software, based on technology from RSA Data Security Inc., requires 309 septillion more times computing power to break the encryption code than Netscape's 40-bit version." Impressive, but the really comforting factor is the competition between software companies, assuring that new versions will give any malicious hacker-thief a strict time limit.

Theft

While the number has been mercifully few, some theft cases have undoubtedly occurred on the Internet. The potential is most certainly there. There's no such thing as an entirely secure system. At least not one that you would want to use! (It would be too involved—and still not totally safe.)

"It lowers the barriers to entry for those people who would defraud," says Rob Bertrum of the North American Securities Administrators Association about the Internet. Marc Beauchamp of NASD says, "You kill 1 fraud and 12 more pop up. It's like a hydra."

Mischief

Recently, hackers broke into the Department of Justice's server and changed its home page into an offensive banner.

Though once again the media blew the event out of proportion (the server was down only a short while), they also (once again) poignantly unearthed a major threat of so-called "open" computer systems. In all cases, the easier it is to use and to communicate, the easier it is to impersonate.

Keys and IDs

The key you see in the lower-left corner of most browsers indicates whether a "digital certificate" security measure is present. This is the current version, but expect to come across variations and enhancements of keys, IDs, and certificates. Keys and IDs are merely a couple of the security measures utilized today.

May I See Your Digital ID?

Digital ID is a brand name from Verisign, which designs digital encryption systems. A solid key indicates that the site itself, but not necessarily you, encodes data transfers. Verisign's site describes them this way: "Digital IDs are the electronic counterparts to driver licenses, passports, and membership cards. A Digital ID can be presented electronically to prove your identity or your right to access information or services online."

There are plenty of other instruments, both now and in development, which will make security precautions on the Web easier *and* more robust. Encryption, coupled with agent technology (which will recognize patterns of use and flag irregularities), is sure to make commerce and trading safer. But there are other issues as well.

Passwords

The omnipresent password may indeed fall by the wayside, but it hasn't happened yet. Machine-to-machine verification systems are on the way, but until then a big security risk occurs with people writing passwords and security codes down, as well as by picking obvious passwords and by repeating passwords. It is indeed easier to remember your password this way, but it makes for poor security. Nonetheless, as it should, convenience outweighs security.

Insurance

The giant companies have already begun to utilize their size by offering various forms of insurance to their customers. This codification of an unspoken rule—that they would stand by their customers—should make life extremely difficult for their competition. At a low enough cost, consumers will choose the added safety of some sort of insurance embellishment.

Fidelity Investments, which has pledged to stand by its investors and investments, will undoubtedly be on the forefront of making its products safer through insurance embellishments.

AT&T already insures purchases on its WorldNet service for its Universal card customers. Given that the Universal card is the second largest issuer of VISAs, expect other credit card companies to follow (they'll have to share the risk with the access provider, though). A news article run around the time of the announcement said of the matter, "[W]hen it comes to Internet transactions, AT&T says the problem is more psychological than financial or technical." Tales of hackers made consumers hesitant to transact business on the Web. However, that has changed rather quickly as the next generation of browsers and security measures have become widespread, and as people become comfortable with the processes.

Regulation

It's indeed amazing that while the Internet has grown from almost nothing into another phone system and more, the regulators have done an admirable job of keeping up. The SEC, in particular, gets kudos for its early and user-friendly presence on the Net. It has let the experiment run; giving occasional direction and warning. An SEC official has said, "Advertising on the Internet is the same thing as advertising in the newspaper, as far as we're concerned." This applies to most everything else, with the exception of the extra slack given the Internet due to its developing status and academic background.

For anyone who feels there may be foul play involved with a site, the Securities and Exchange Commission has an Enforcement Complaint Center, "a link to an electronic mailbox that enables the public to communicate directly with the SEC's Division of Enforcement regarding possible instances of securities fraud." Located at http://www.sec.gov/enforce/comctr.htm, the SEC says, "the Center features a simple, understandable form that the user can complete and send to the Enforcement Division with the click of a mouse. The Enforcement Complaint Center can also be reached through the SEC's home page at `http://www.sec.gov`." Commission staff members (including those from both the Division of Enforcement and the Office of Investor Education and Assistance) review every message sent to the center, and it accepts any types of fraud complaints (not just those relating to the Internet).

"There exists a remarkable culture of self-policing by individual Internet users who resent the intrusion of the crooks and thieves trying to exploit this new medium," says William McLucas, the Director of the Division of Enforcement. "We hope to tap into this culture, encouraging users to let us know of dubious offerings on the World Wide Web or suspicious postings on the many usenet groups and bulletin boards.

"By reporting suspected instances of fraudulent activity relating to securities, a user acts not only to help himself, but also to prevent losses by other investors." McLucas adds, "If you believe that you have been the victim of a securities-related fraud, through the Internet or otherwise, or if you believe that any person or entity may have violated or is currently violating the federal securities laws, we would like to hear from you."

The Enforcement Complaint Center provides an Enforcement Internet Fraud Hotline and several helpful booklets. Below is an excerpt from the SEC's "Investment Fraud and Abuse Travel to Cyberspace" publication:

The Online Investment Scam:
New Medium, Same Message

While investment con-artists have been quick to seize upon on-line computing as a new way to cheat investors, the types of investment fraud seen on-line mirror frauds perpetrated over the phone or through the mail. Consider all offers with skepticism. Investment frauds usually fit one of the following categories:

The Pyramid

*"How To Make Big Money From Your Home Computer!!!"
One on-line promoter claimed recently that you could "turn $5
into $60,000 in just three to six weeks." In reality, this program
was just an electronic version of the classic "pyramid" scheme
in which participants attempt to make money solely by recruit-
ing new participants into the program. This type of fraud is
well-suited for the world of on-line computing where a trouble-
maker can easily send messages to a thousand people with the
touch of a button. Unfortunately, these "investment opportunities" collapse when no new "investors" can be found.*

The Risk-Free Fraud

*"Exciting, Low-Risk Investment Opportunities" to partici-
pate in exotic-sounding investments, including wireless cable
projects, prime bank securities and eel farms, have been offered
on-line. One promoter attempted to get people to invest in a
fictitious coconut plantation in Costa Rica, claiming the
investment was "similar to a C.D., with a better interest
rate." Promoters misrepresent the risk by comparing their
offer to something safe, like bank certificates of deposit.
Sometimes, an investment product does not even exist -
they're scams.*

The "Pump and Dump" Scam

*It is common to see messages posted on-line urging readers to
buy a stock quickly that is poised for rapid growth, or telling
you to sell before it goes down. Often the writer claims to have
"inside" information about an impending development, or will
claim to use an "infallible" combination of economic and stock
market data to pick stocks. In reality, the promoter may be an
insider who stands to gain by selling shares after the stock price
is pumped up by gullible investors, or a short seller who stands
to gain if the price goes down. This ploy may be used with lit-
tle-known, thinly traded stocks.*

The SEC Is Tracking Fraud

In investigating on-line fraud, the SEC can get a court order to stop scams. The SEC took action in the following cases:

Pleasure Time, Inc: Astronomical profits were promised in a worldwide telephone lottery. Over two million dollars of unregistered securities were sold to 20,000 investors who were encouraged to recruit other investors on the Internet. The SEC filed a lawsuit and the company's assets were frozen.

IVT Systems: The company solicited investments to finance the construction of an ethanol plant in the Dominican Republic. The Internet solicitations promised a return of 50% or more with no reasonable basis for the prediction. Their literature contained lies about contracts with well known companies and omitted other important information for investors. After the SEC filed a complaint, they agreed to stop breaking the law.

Scott Frye posted a notice that he was looking for investors for two Costa Rican companies that produced coconut chips. He claimed A&P supermarkets placed an order to buy all the chips he could produce. He was forced to withdraw his notice when his lies were discovered.

Gene Block and Renate Haag were caught offering "prime bank" securities, a type of security that doesn't even exist. They collected over $3.5 million by promising to double investors' money in four months. The SEC has frozen their assets and stopped them from continuing their fraud.

Daniel Odulo was stopped from soliciting investors for a proposed eel farm. Odulo promised investors a "whopping 20% return," claiming that the investment was "low risk." When he was caught by the SEC, he consented to the court order stopping him from breaking the securities laws.

Here's How You Can Protect Yourself

Follow our checklist and you should steer clear of on-line fraud, but first a word about the information these companies are required to file at the SEC and some basic tips.

The SEC does not require companies that are raising less than one million dollars to be "registered" at the SEC, but these companies are required to file a "Form D" with the SEC. The Form D is a brief notice which includes the names and addresses of owners and promoters, but little other information. Call the SEC at (202) 942-8090 to get a copy of the Form D. If there isn't a Form D, call the SEC's Office of Investor Education and Assistance at (202) 942-7040. But don't stop there. You should always check with your state securities regulator to see if they have more information about the company and the people behind it, and if your state regulator has cleared the offering for sale in your state.

Because these small companies are usually the most risky investments that you can make, you should always get as much written information as you can from the company. Check out this information with an unbiased and informed source – your broker, accountant or lawyer. Your state's securities regulator should be your first stop, but you may also want to visit your local library and talk with the librarian about other sources of information. There are a number of services that provide a constant stream of information about the financial condition of companies. Make sure you know as much as possible about the company, before you invest. Don't ever rely solely on what you read on-line to make an investment decision.

As you can see from the above, the SEC is definitely on the case. However, common sense is always the best protection; don't send money (or even information) to anyone you don't know. Period.

Next, the NASD, or National Association of Securities Dealers (i.e., stockbrokers) also has a complaint center. Its NASD Regulation Inc. subsidiary launched a site (www.nsadr.com) that has brochures and other anti-fraud literature. They warn specifically against online investment "tips" and stock touting. While it is useful to have these regulatory resources available, common sense and healthy skepticism should be enough to protect you.

A Dow Jones Business News article on the NASD's online offerings said, "For its part, the NASD is paying closer attention to cyberspace stock chat. 'We do have a team that is surfing the Internet,' and checking out on-line discussions of companies that trade on Nasdaq," says [Mary] Schapiro. They're far more concerned about stock manipulation than fund manipulation, which is almost impossible to do.

Just as in the paper world you shouldn't send large checks to an organization you haven't investigated at least somewhat. Don't transfer money on the Internet without double-checking that you're dealing with a reputable organization. And take it slow.

Digital Privacy

Another much talked-about area is privacy. How much information is available to companies with which you transact, and how much of your personal information is available to other individuals on the Web? Plenty. But privacy issues on the Web, too, have been overblown. Sure, information will be available on every detail of your life, but this is already the case.

When visiting a Web site, the site can already tell your domain name (the part following the @ sign). But some sites also can tell where you're visiting, by way of a file called a "cookie," which records sections of a site. Though they can't tell any further specific information about you, they can tell that you're a single machine and which areas you've visited.

As we've seen, the best privacy protection up to now has been sheer volume. Mischievous sorts have just too much to choose from. Most people have enough trouble handling the daily information coming across their desks; they don't have any time to seek out someone else's private information. And, even if they do, finding it is another matter.

Just be aware, be careful, and keep a low profile. These are the best defenses.

History of Internet Schemes

The SEC's listings above covered several of the well-publicized cases of fraud, but I want to examine these in further detail. I also want to expand their list, to make it a comprehensive "Internet investment schemes" chronology. In each of these cases, the adage "if it's too good to be true, it probably is" would've saved these investors' money.

Pyramid Schemes—Fortuna

Among other schemes already uncovered by regulators, one of the first involved Fortuna Alliance L.L.C. (limited liability corporation). This Bellingham, Washington, company was operating a traditional "pyramid scheme"—where new investors are needed to pay out unrealistic rates of return to previous investors. It enticed investors through its World Wide Web site with promises of outrageous returns, made possible through the use of a "mystical mathematical formula" developed by the Fibonacci (of sequence fame). The site mentioned charitable activities and "new age" products, but these apparently were merely a cover.

The FTC (Federal Trade Commission) put a stop to this company's activities in May 1995, alleging unfair and deceptive trade practices. Fortuna had taken in more than $6 million from as many as 30,000 investors. The moral of the story of this, and of any investment "idea" that sounds like a pyramid scheme, is this: if it sounds too good to be true or legal, it is.

Other Cases

As mentioned, Pleasure Time, Inc., a company operating out of Ohio, offered investors huge profits from a "worldwide telephone lottery." The company supposedly offered unregistered securities to about 20,000 people and raised more than $3 million. This was one of the SEC's first high-profile prosecutions of scams on the Internet, but it certainly won't be its last.

Most schemes such as these, which follow the classic Ponzi scheme pattern, involve either "penny stocks" or exotic investments. Thus, the easiest way to avoid them is to not invest in them at all. This is why I suggest investing *only* in large, reputable no-load mutual fund companies. You may give up some returns somewhere along the line, but you also may well protect your investment dollars from being lured away to some Caribbean island.

Other Dangers

"Everybody thinks cyberspace is the wild frontier, but in terms of defamation, the laws are not that much different," notes Michael Sullivan, at the law firm Ross, Dixon, and Masbach in Washington, D.C. "The courts have applied the same rules" on the Internet as elsewhere.

I've mentioned my aversion to recommending individual stocks for most smaller investors. While in the past there has always been the chance of foul play on the part of management or Wall Street, with the spread of the electronic bulletin board, there comes another risk: the technically-savvy but green-to-investments "anonymous" tip. I told you the story of Iomega, the disk drive maker, in the section on America Online's *The Motley Fool*, but I wanted to add a couple of other cautionary tales from here and elsewhere on the Web.

Diana Corporation is another stock that was "born on the Internet." While investment bankers laughed at its prospects, bulletin board enthusiasts began honing in on this Milwaukee-based meat and seafood company turned

Internet-switch technology stock. Shares soared and plunged as first supporters, then detractors gained the upper hand in BBS discussions. Even accusations of Securities and Exchange Commission investigations, which turned out to be false at first (but which also quickly got the attention of the Commission), turned up online.

Other cases of online comments affecting stocks dramatically include the following stories.

Presstek

Though this printing company's fortunes were also tied to the investment newsletter industry (specifically, Carlton Lutts' Cabot Market Letter), its online following clearly was a large factor in this stocks' meteoric rise ... and crash back to earth.

Guardian Insurance Financial Services

A tiny electronic newsletter entitled "Wacco Kid Hot Stocks Forum," which is run by amateur investor Gayle Essary, picked this and other "penny stocks" and watched them rise dramatically. However, following an initial jump, prices in many of these highly speculative companies have turned sour.

A *Business Week* article quoted one online participant, "We publicize the stock on the boards [investment newsgroups], and the price goes up." Avoid involvement with this sort of manipulation at all costs. Not only is it probably illegal, it is a most dangerous way of investing as well. This same article quoted HealthTech International's (affected by one of the online "buys") President Tim Williams about the online forum. On the Wacco Kid he says, "They're acutely aware of the power of the tool itself."

The Motley Fool's producer Keith Pelczarski was quoted as saying, "The last thing we want to do is to become a device that some huckster uses to dupe people out of their money." The Fools may have started out as an honest exchange of investing ideas, but the opportunity for manipulation has become too great. Not only do you now have to be aware of brokers, but even honest engineers may be way off base as far as investments go. Just knowing that a product is good isn't enough anymore.

Though initial investors who get out of these schemes or highflying investments in time probably make spectacular profits, many are based on either luck or illegal activities. You don't want to base your investment decisions on either, or be involved in either case. As in the real world, people with vested interests in both the success or failure (via short-selling, or betting on a decline in prices) of a company tend to overly hype their side of the story. The small investor must be extra careful, particularly when it comes to comments made online. Thankfully, mutual funds are mostly immune to this kind of manipulation.

Bob Metcalfe, a columnist of *InfoWorld* magazine, has stated that, "You've read that the Internet was designed to survive thermonuclear war, but it has repeatedly been brought to its knees, its circuits choked," by too many users. He states that the Internet will "go supernova" and "catastrophically collapse" because of the volume of usage. While most Web users consider this a major overstatement, it certainly remains a possibility.

Of course, the threat of the Internet collapsing is a very real one, and investors, in particular, should consider the implications should this occur. You should be prepared to use the phone first of all, especially if you were in the middle of an online transaction. Clarifying whether a "buy" went through is your first step—you don't want to blindly enter a transaction again else you could wind up buying two whatevers.

The Future of Investing on the Internet

It is, of course, impossible to predict how exactly the future of online investing will develop, to say the least. But it will be exciting and interesting to watch. Please keep in mind that this book was written in late 1996, so some of the material, especially the addresses, may need updating. We're providing an address for readers to give feedback and to update their URL lists.

Please feel free to e-mail me at:

pcrane1@ix.netcom.com

and I will send you an updated URL list.

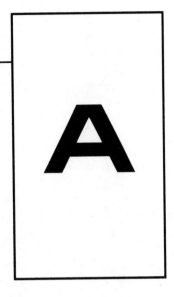

Bookmarks by Chapter

Chapter 4-6

Cyberglossary on page 110

Chapter 7

Online Service/Internet Service Provider Sites

AT&T	http://www.att.com
Netcom Online	http://www.netcom.com

GNN	http://www.gnn.com
America Online	http://www.aol.com
Prodigy	http://www.prodigy.com
Compuserve	http://www.compuserve.com

Chapter 8

Search Sites

Yahoo	http://www.yahoo.com
Alta Vista	http://www.altavista.com
	http://www.altavista.digital.com
HotBot	http://www.hotbot.com
Excite	http://www.excite.com
Lycos	http://www.lycos.com
Point	*http://www.point.com*
A2Z	*http://a2z.lycos.com/*
Infoseek	http://www.infoseek.com
Open Text	http://index.opentext.net
WebCrawler	http://webcrawler.com
Magellan	http://www.mckinley.com
Search.com	http://www.search.com
InfoSpace	http://www.infospace.com
Starting Point—Investing	http://www.stpt.com/ invest.html

Chapter 9

News Sites

Wall Street Journal IE	http://wsj.com
USA Today—Money News	http://www.usatoday.com/money
NY Times on the Web	http://www.nytimes.com
Investor's Business Daily	http://www.ibd.com
CNNfn	http://www.cnnfn.com
MSNBC	http://www.msnbc.com
CNBC	http://www.cnbc.com
Bloomberg	http://www.bloomberg.com
Reuters	http://www.reuters.com
iGuide—Money & Careers	http://www.iguide.com/work_mny/index.sml
LeadStory	http://www.leadstory.com
Boston Globe Online Business	http://www.boston.com/globe
WashingtonPost.com	http://www.washingtonpost.com
San Jose Mercury News	http://www.sjmercury.com
Individual's NewsPage	http://www.newspage.com
PointCast Network	http://www.pointcast.com
IBM's InfoSage	http://www.infosage.ibm.com

Magazine Sites

Barron's Online	http://www.barrons.com
Money Magazine Online	http://pathfinder.com
Fortune/Time/Etc.	http://pathfinder.com
Mutual Funds Magazine Online	http://www.mfmag.com
Worth OnLine	http://www.worth.com
Kiplinger's OnLine	http://www.kiplinger.com
Forbes Magazine	http://www.forbes.com
Research Magazine Online	http://www.researchmag.com
U.S. News Online	http://www.usnews.com
Green Magazine	http://members.aol.com/greenzine

Chapter 10

"The Big 3" Fund Company Sites

Fidelity Investments	http://www.fid-inv.com
Charles Schwab & Co.	http://www.schwab.com
Vanguard Group	http://www.vanguard.com

Chapter 11

No-Load and Other Mutual Fund Sites

NETworth by GALT Technologies	http://networth.galt.com
AAII	*http://www.aaii.org*
T. Rowe Price	http://www.troweprice.com
Dreyfus	http://www.dreyfus.com
Scudder No-Load Funds	http://funds.scudder.com
Twentieth Century Mutual Funds	http://www.twentieth-century.com
Twentieth Century on NETWorth	*http://networth.galt.com/www/home/mutual/twntyth/twntyth*
The Benham Group	*http://networth.galt.com/benham/benham*
Janus Funds	http://www.janusfunds.com
Janus on NETWorth	*http://networth.galt.com/www/home/mutual/janus*
Strong Funds	http://www.strong-funds.com
Invesco	http://www.invesco.com
Stein Roe Mutual Funds	http://networth.galt.com/www/home/mutual/steinroe
Liberty Financial Companies	*http://www.lib.com*
Montgomery Funds	http://networth.galt.com/www/home/mutual/mntgmry/mntgmry

Montgomery Securities	*http://www.montgomery.com*
IAI Mutual Funds	http://networth.galt.com/iai
Robertson Stephens & Co.	http://www.rsim.com
Calvert Group Home Page	http://www.calvertgroup.com
Gabelli Funds	http://www.gabelli.com
GIT Funds	http://www.gitfunds.com
SAFECO Mutual Funds	http://networth.galt.com/ www/home/mutual/safeco

Additional Sites Not Included in Text

Mutual Fund Co. Directory @ CMU	*http://www.cs.cmu.edu/ ~jdg/funds/us.html*
Crabbe Huson Funds	http://www.contrarian.com
Oakmark Funds	http://networth.galt.com/www/ home/mutual/100/oakmark
PBHG Funds	http://networth.galt.com/ www/home/mutual/pbhg
United Services Funds	http://www.usfunds.com

Chapter 12

Discount Brokers

PAWWS Financial Network	http://pawws.com

Jack White & Company	http://pawws.com/jwc
National Discount Broker	http://pawws.com/ndb
The Net Investor	http://pawws.com/tni
Lombard Securities	http://www.lombard.com
E*Trade	http://www.etrade.com
Quick & Reilly On-line	http://www.quick&reilly.com
OLDE Discount Corporation	http://www.oldenet.com
PC Financial Network	http://www.pcfn.com
Accutrade Home Page	http://www.accutrade.com
K. Aufhauser's WealthWeb	http://www.aufhauser.com
CompuTEL Securities	http://www.rapidtrade.com
Ceres Securities	http://www.ceres.com
eBroker	http://www.ebroker.com
Discount Broker Listing— NCII	*http://com.primenet.com/ncii/links*

Full Service Brokers

A.G. Edwards	http://www.agedwards.com
Goldman Sachs	http://www.gs.com
Gruntal & Co.	http://www.gruntal.com
Hambrecht & Quist	http://www.hamquist.com
Kemper Funds	http://www.kemper.com
Legg Mason	http://www.leggmason.com
Merrill Lynch	http://www.ml.com

Morgan Stanley	http://www.ms.com
Prudential Securities	http://www.prusec.com
Smith Barney	http://nestegg.iddis.com/smithbarney

Chapter 13

Information on Funds and Investing

INVESTools	http://investools.com
Mutual Funds Interactive	http://www.brill.com
IDD's Nest Egg	http://nestegg.iddis.com
Nest Egg's WebFinance	*http://nestegg.iddis.com/webfinance*
Mutual Fund Education Assoc.	http://www.mfea.com
InvestorGuide Finance MegaCenter	http://www.investorguide.com
InvestorGuide Mutual Funds	*http://www.investorguide.com/MutualFunds*
Quicken Financial Network	http://www.qfn.com
Mutual Fund Research	http://www.webcom.com/fundlink
IBC Financial Data	http://www.ibcdata.com
IBC's MFII Page	*http://www.ibcdata.com/mfii*

GNN's Personal Finance Center	http://www.gnn.com/gnn/meta/finance
Thomson MarketEdge	http://www.marketedge.com
Reuters Money Network	http://www.rmn.com
Briefing by Charter Media	http://www.briefing.com
WallStreetWeb by BulletProof	http://www.bulletproof.com
DBC (Data Broadcasting Corp.)	http://www.dbc.com
The Finance Center	http://www.tfc.com
The Syndicate	http://www.moneypages.com/syndicate
Wall Street City	http://www.wallstreetcity.com
FinanceHub	http://www.financehub.com
Research Magazine	http://www.researchmag.com
Stock Smart	http://www.stocksmart.com
Investor's Edge	http://www.irnet.com
Fundscape	http://fundscape.com
Mutual Fund Café	http://www.mfcafe.com
Bonds Online	http://www.bondsonline.com
Money Talks	http://www.talks.com
1-800-Mutuals	http://www.1800mutuals.com

Quotes and Information on Stocks

PC Quote	http://www.pcquote.com
QuoteCom	http://www.quote.com

Wall Street Online	http://www.wso.com
The Motley Fool	http://fool.web.aol.com//fool_mn
Netstock Direct (DRIPs)	http://www.netstockdirect.com
Silicon Investor	http://www.techstocks.com
Stockmaster	http://www.stockmaster.com
Equis	http://www.equis.com

Additional Sites Not Included in Text

Kuber's Trading Desk	http://www.best.com/~mwahal/invest
NYSE	http://www.nyse.com
The Nasdaq Stock Market	http://www.nasdaq.com
The Financial Data Finder	http://www.cob.ohio-state.edu/dept/fin/osudata
Invest-o-rama!	http://www.investorama.com
Money Pages	http://www.moneypages.com
NAIC Home Page	http://www.better-investing.org
Wall Street Research Net	http://www.wsrn.com
Welcome to the 401k Forum	http://www.401kforum.com
Welcome to the TIPnet Home Page	http://www.tipnet.com
Financenter	http://www.financenter.com
INVEST$LINK	http://www.imfnet.com/pitbull/links1

Xplore Investing	http://www.xplore.com/xplore500/medium/investing

Chapter 14

Personal Finance Resources

Banking

Bank Rate Monitor	http://www.brm.com
Security First Network Bank	http://www.sfnb.com
First Chicago NBD Corporation	http://www.fcnbd.com
Bank of America	http://www.bankamerica.com
J.P. Morgan	http://www.jpmorgan.com
Fleet	http://www.fleet.com
NationsBank	http://www.nationsbank.com
PNC's Compass Funds	http://www.compassfunds.com
Wells Fargo (Stagecoach Funds)	http://www.wellsfargo.com

Taxes

Internal Revenue Service	http://www.irs.ustreas.gov
Internal Revenue Code	http://mip.ups-tlse.fr/~grundman/ustax/www/contents

AICPA	http://www.rutgers.edu/Accounting/raw/aicpa/home
ABA Tax Section	http://www.abanet.org/tax/home
Net Taxes	http://www.ypn.com/taxes
Intuit's TurboTax Online	http://www.intuit.com/turbotax

Government

EDGAR (SEC)	http://www.townhall.org/edgar/edgar
NYU EDGAR Development Site	*http://edgar.stern.nyu.edu*
Disclosure (private SEC data co.)	http://www.disclosure.com
U.S. Treasury	http://www.ustreas.gov/treasury
U.S. Dept. of Commerce	http://www.doc.gov
Commerce Dept's Stat USA Site	http://www.stat-usa.gov
U.S. Dept. of Labor	http://www.dol.gov
U.S. Congress "Thomas"	http://thomas.loc.gov
U.S. Postal Service Scam Tips	http://www.usps.gov/websites/depart/inspect
Federal Reserve of St. Louis	http://www.stls.frb.org/fred

Economics

FINWeb WWW Server	http://www.finweb.com

Ohio St. Finance Links	http://www.cob.ohio-state.edu/dept/fin/overview

Insurance

Best of America variable annuities	http://www.boa.com
Nationwide	http://www.nationwide.com

Additional Sites Not Included in Text

InsWeb - Insurance On-Line	http://www.insweb.com
MetLife	http://www.metlife.com
Welcome to GEICO Home Page	http://www.geico.com/home
Insurance News Network	http://www.insure.com
Quicken InsureMarket Home Page	http://www.insuremarket.com
The Economic Briefing Room	http://www.whitehouse.gov/fsbr/esbr

Chapter 16

Regulation

SEC Division of Enforcement	http://www.sec.gov/enforce/comctr

| Securities & Exchange Commission | http://www.sec.gov/index |
| Consumer Information Center | http://www.pueblo.gsa.gov |

ADDITIONAL URLs

Investing Basics/Readings

100% No-Load Council	http://networth.galt.com/www/home/mutual/100/100guide
AAII—Computer Investing Basics	http://www.aaii.org/ci/cibasic1
Fleet—Investing Primer	http://www.fleet.com/abtyou/persinv/primer
How to Pick a Fund	http://www.elibrary.com/intuit/10030
Indexing advocate	http://www.cob.ohio-state.edu/~fin/cern/under
PAWWS On Mutual Fund Investing	http://pawws.secapl.com/Mfis_phtml/mf06
Vangd—Stock Market Volatility	http://www.vanguard.com/new/investor/II19960715A
Vangd—Tracking Newspaper Lists	http://www.vanguard.com/educ/module1/m1_8_0
Vangd Recommended Reading	http://www.vanguard.com/educ/module1/m1_rr.html
Vanguard Literature Library	http://www.vanguard.com/catalog/5_4

Links & Lists

DBC Online Suggested Links	http://www.dbc.com/cgi-bin/htx.exe/dbcc/links.html?SOURCE=DBCC
Finance Library	http://www.cob.ohio-state.edu/dept/fin/overview.htm
GNN Select Personal Finance	http://nearnet.gnn.com/gnn/wic/wics/persfin.funds.html
iGuide Net Reviews— MONEY	http://www.iguide.com/insites/9/
Industry Web Sites	http://www.dbcams.com/resource.htm
InvestorGuide Mutual Funds	http://www.investorguide.com/MutualFunds.htm#linklists
Manhattanlink' Sites	http://www.manhattanlink.com/other.htm
Money Favorites	http://pathfinder.com/@@XdH@2gUA4toATT7C/money/websites/latestwebsites
Moneyline—Links	http://www.moneyline.com/mlc_lnk1.html
NCII—List of Sites	http://com.primenet.com/ncii/other.html
Netscape Finance	http://home.netscape.com/escapes/finance/index.html
NYT—Business Connections	http://www.nytimes.com/library/cyber/reference/busconn
SEC's Other Sites	http://www.sec.gov/others.htm

Syndicate—Mutual Funds	http://www.itlnet.com/moneypages/syndicate/mfunds/funds
Telesphere's Sites—Intl	http://www.telesph.com/sites.html
Wall Street Directory, Inc.	http://www.wsdinc.com/index.html

A final note: These URLs are, of course, subject to change. I will be providing an updated listing at the following site:

http://www.netcom.com/~pcrane1/mfii

Please e-mail me at: *pcrane1@ix.netcom.com* with suggestions, additions, or comments.

Bibliography

Graham, Ian S., "HTML Sourcebook," Wiley Computer Publishing. 1996.

Malkiel, Burton, "A Random Walk Down Wall Street," W.W. Norton & Co. 1990.

Lichty, Tom, "The Official America Online Tour Guide," Ventana. 1996.

Related Works

Allrich, Ted, "The On-Line Investor: How to Find the Best Stocks Using Your Computer," St. Martin's Press. 1995

Brown, David L., and Kassandra Bentley, "Cyber Investing: Cracking Wall Street With Your Personal Computer," John Wiley & Sons. 1995.

Dettmann, Terry R., and Susan Futterman, "Using CompuServe to Make You Rich," Waite Group Press. 1996.

Farrell, Paul B., "Investor's Guide to the Net: Making Money Online," John Wiley & Sons. 1996.

Fister, Mark, "Money on the Internet," Sybex. 1995.

Gardner, David and Tom, "The Motley Fool Investment Guide," Simon & Schuster. 1996.

Goldstein, Douglas, and Joyce Flory, "The Online Guide to Personal Finance and Investing,"

Irwin Professional Publishing. 1996.

Jubak, Jim, "The Worth Guide to Computerized Investing: Everything You Need to Know to Use

Your Home Computer to Make More Money in the Stock Market," S&S. 1996.

Schwabach, Robert "The Business Week Guide to Global Investments Using Electronic Tools," Osbourne McGraw-Hill. 1994.

Wayner, Peter, "Digital Cash," AP Professional. 1996.

Index

B

C

D